OFF THE BEATEN CART PATH

Off the Beaten Cart Path

Uncovering the Stories of America's Little Known, but Beloved, Golf Courses

DAVE MARRANDETTE

WILEY

John Wiley & Sons, Inc.

Published by John Wiley & Sons, Inc., Hoboken, New Jersey
Published simultaneously in Canada

For general information on our other products and services or for technical support, please contact our Customer Care Department within the United States at (800) 762-2974, outside the United States at (317) 572-3993 or fax (317) 572-4002.

Wiley also publishes its books in a variety of electronic formats. Some content that appears in print may not be available in electronic books. For more information about Wiley products, visit our web site at www.wiley.com.

Library of Congress Cataloging-in-Publication Data:

Marrandette, Dave G., 1947-
  Off the beaten cart path / Dave Marrandette
          p. cm.
  Includes bibliographical references and index.
ISBN-13 978-0-471-97997-5 (cloth.)
ISBN-10 0-471-97997-X (cloth)
  1.Golf courses – United States. 2. Golf courses – United States – Anecdotes. I. Title.
  GV981.M287 2006
  796.352'06873—dc22

                                2006042643

Printed in the United States of America

10 9 8 7 6 5 4 3 2 1

Contents

OFF THE BEATEN CART PATH

Introduction

EVERY GOLF COURSE HAS A STORY

Thanks to the National Golf Foundation and Golf Datatech, organizations that have taken it upon themselves to crunch the numbers, we know that there are approximately sixteen thousand golf courses in the United States and another fifteen thousand other golfing facilities—driving ranges or dedicated practice and learning centers. Of these sixteen thousand golf courses, the majority are *Off the Beaten Cart Path.* They are away from major metropolitan areas. They are not part of the scheme of a golf resort. They are not a stop on a golf trail. They are not included in a golf factory's facilities. Some are located just a five iron or so off an Interstate, but in small communities where you would hardly expect to find such gems. Others are miles away from a major highway and require a little research and a good map to find.

Every one of these courses has a story. Each one has a tale to tell, some secret to share, a hidden or obvious nuance that will lure you to its first tee. It is not just the Augusta

Nationals or the Pebble Beaches or the Pine Valleys that have entertaining and fascinating histories behind them. To the golfing enthusiast, every golf course becomes a living, breathing entity that takes on a life of its own and develops a history. There may be a great story about the course's origin—perhaps part myth or part legend, but always founded in truth. But the account of why the golf gods decided to breathe life into a particular course in an prescribed place at a certain moment in time always exists. The course may have colorful anecdotes about the characters that have walked its fairways: the eccentric, the powerful, the dedicated, the professional—and the inept. A golf course may have comic or tragic epics to reveal, events from aces to albatrosses that have transpired on its tees and greens. In every clubhouse you'll find an anecdote or a memory that makes each and every course distinctive, a story that gives each owner, member, and regular player pride in his or her local golf course. But for whatever reason a golf course beckons to us, we ought to listen for those tales that make each golf course special.

And just like each golfer, every golf course has a personality all its own, those peculiar characteristics and eccentric qualities that are representative of and particular to that course. The layout, the condition, the scenery, the history, the people, and even the price all have a direct influence on its personality. The sum of these qualities makes a golf course what it is. Think of it: we form an opinion of every golf course that we play. Through our experience with a course, we determine our feeling for it. That impression is a result of most or all of these factors. As we play the course, we discover the personality and develop certain feelings for it—a direct result of that personality. The more we play a course, the more we uncover its personality and the more intimate with it we become.

The philosophers of the links, those scribes who attempt to capture the spirit of the game from ivory towers and expensive resorts, tell us that golf is a microcosm of life. The fact is they are correct, even if they understand only half of the reason why. They believe each golfer's character is revealed as he or she plays the game. But part of that revelation is a direct result of all golfers' reactions to the personality of the golf courses they play. Without its own distinct personality, the course could not test the character of the golfer. Everybody that we meet in our journeys through life has a unique personality and each, in turn, reacts differently to everybody that he or she meets. It is the same with golf courses. As we play a course we respond to it and reveal our own characters. And we respond differently to each course we play.

To modify the philosophy of Forrest Gump's mother, discovering golf courses is like a box of chocolates: they're all good; they just each have a different flavor. You never know what the filling is going to be until you take the first bite. But you must take that first bite; you must play that first hole. And never judge a golf course by its "cover," the overall panoramic view that you get from the first tee. There will always be a sweet delight inside, great holes to be played, and unexpected challenges ahead. There are always secrets to be discovered.

So if you follow this philosophy, you should delve into every golf course that you come upon and take great delight in it. I have played golf for over forty-eight years, and

I've never met a golf course I didn't like. That's true Gump philosophy. Some, of course, I like better than others. Though they may look similar on the outside, with tees, fairways, greens, bunkers, water, and the like, each has a distinct flavor. Once you get to the core of a course, each one entices your golfing taste buds with its own extraordinary zest. Some will get your attention with the beauty of their surroundings. There is beauty in the mountains, in the deserts, in the pine forests, and on the links. Each course exudes its own unique attractiveness. Some will seduce you with their layouts, carefully crafted to lure you into making critical decisions that will affect your score. You must decide: go for the green or lay up safely? Cut the corner or play free from harm? Perhaps a course prides itself on its customer service. Warm feelings emanate from a course where everyone is greeted with a smile and common courtesy reigns regardless of the price you pay or its reputation. Perhaps a course has a well-deserved history. But you must play the course, walking in the footsteps of the greats, to gain a true appreciation of their trials and tribulations. It is only then that you will totally comprehend the romance of the course.

The courses that appeal to us the most are the backbone of American golf: the undistinguished, often nine-hole courses located in the towns, villages, and hamlets across the country. The heart and soul of the game in the United States is not at the opulent and overpriced golf resorts, the places where the emphasis is on the business of golf and where making a profit is the sole reason for being. This is where the 70-hour workweek of the golf professional isn't as important as last month's bottom line. This is where you'll find the money, along with the ivory towers of the game and the professional tours, but it is not where the game is truly played. You won't locate the heart and soul of the game at another tournament players club built at a cost of $12 million. Rather, you need to look in the back room of an adobe-style clubhouse in Van Horn, Texas, where two friends, one African American and one Mexican American, are watching a golf tournament on a small television mounted in a corner of the room. But when you walk in to gather information about the course and inquire about the possibility of playing, you get their undivided attention and a glad-to-have-you-here attitude. It is there that you will find a used-club barrel containing a couple of old persimmon woods that you can purchase for a dollar or two.

The folks who own, operate, manage, or just take care of these local golf courses are the ones who are truly responsible for the upkeep of the game in the United States. Don't believe all the hoopla on television. It's on community courses like the one found in Beaver, Utah, where the local high school golf team has a place to practice and play, where young men and young women can dream of challenging Tiger or Phil or Ernie for the United States Open. It's the nine-hole courses like the one found in Chamberlain, South Dakota, where you'll find an inscribed bench dedicated to Joe Scales, who was still winning club championships in 2001 at the age of sixty-five before he went on to greener fairways. And "one of the best nine-hole courses in Texas" can be found in Sonora, Texas: just check the sign attesting to that fact next to the sixth tee.

These are the American golf courses at which the membership is like a family—an extended family, if you will. Every member of that family takes great pride in his or her course regardless of its ranking (or, usually, lack of ranking) in a national golf magazine. All those stars handed out so generously and all those lists of great places to play mean nothing. This course is ours, we are family, and that's all that matters. Many will play no other course in their lives. They are content to traverse the fairways of home and appreciate the subtle nuances that familiarity affords. These are memberships that honor their deceased comrades, as at Rio Mimbres Golf Course in Deming, New Mexico. On the fifteenth tee sits a marker in memory of John Stewart, a longtime member of the club. The marker is captioned, "This is the only tree I never hit," a tree that was planted after his passing.

It is easy for all of us to find any number of reasons to dislike a golf course, but we can always find at least one reason to take pleasure in its personality. Regardless of the condition, regardless of the location, regardless of the length of the round, regardless of the attitude of the staff, there will always be an incentive to like a golf course. To find that reason, you may be forced to talk to other golfers—perhaps experience a round with one in a pair of shorts and a T-shirt.

One note of caution: if you cannot find a reason, it may, sadly, be time to hang up the clubs. You could be contracting a terminal case of golf snobbery. Such an ailment is contagious, and you will not be allowed to play the game on any course with any other players. Adopt the motto, "I never met a course I didn't like." You will never be disappointed.

First impressions of a golf course often permanently determine our opinions about it. One of the first perspectives we get about a golf course is its scorecard: you can always get a reliable initial perception of a course simply by reading it. Read and observe the entire card, not just the course's basic statistics. Read the local rules, read the advertisements, and look at the pictures. If you pay attention you might even find a coupon for a free hamburger or an oil change. The scorecard will enhance your appetite for the golf course. It will let you know what you're in for and give you the proper attitude for your round.

Experience is a major buzzword at golf facilities today. The owners and staff want you to have a good experience at their course. You, of course, want to have a good experience, too. The total golfing experience is based on many factors. But certainly one of those factors is the story of the course. Someone at every golf course you play knows about its history. If you know how a golf course came into existence, you will have a greater appreciation for the course, and a better overall experience.

The courses we found reflect the architectural style of the time they were created. While it may be a bit of an oversimplification, golf architecture basically falls into two time periods. The golden age of golf course architecture can be found in the old style links built in the 1920s and 1930s, although some were designed as late as the 1940s and early 1950s. These designs feature courses by Donald Ross, Alister MacKenzie, and others. Representative of the modern style courses from the latter half of the twentieth century are courses by Pete Dye, Robert Trent Jones, and a host of other modern architects. These two architectural periods are distinguished by certain characteristics. And while there is more to golf architecture than short or long, or wide open or narrow, these features usually set the two periods apart.

Shorter, narrower golf courses are typical of the old style architecture. They didn't need to be long. The equipment was different from today's, and the ball didn't travel as far: the focus was on accuracy, not distance. Modern courses tend to be longer but more wide open. This architectural style is partly a reflection of the equipment available in today's golf world. Neither style is better than the other. They both have their merits. What is wonderful is that you can find eighteen-hole courses today that have a mixture of both. Bear Creek in Forest City, Iowa, is one. The front nine were constructed in the early 1950s, and the back nine in 2003. The end result is that you get to play a course that has two totally different styles of architecture. Bear Creek and many others like it are a treat to play. They give you a taste of the old and a taste of the new, and challenge your game in new ways.

EVERY BOOK HAS A STORY

Behind every book is also a story, a tale of how the volume came into being. It is not the blood, sweat, and tears, not the hours of research, writing, editing, and rewriting. Certainly these are a component of the process, but they are common to every book written. Rather, the story is in the inspiration. There is a moment when an author receives a literary revelation, an idea is sparked, and the work begins. There is an instant before the project begins that the author realizes the worthiness of the undertaking.

This volume is no different. It was forged from two concurrent happenings: constant travel during the last four years and playing countless numbers of golf courses that you will not find listed in the major golf publications—or anywhere else, for that matter. Gathering together all the information necessary for this book has been an ongoing pursuit for those four years. The project has been a labor of love. But it has been more than that. It's more than simply four years of actual research that you'll find within these pages. It's forty-eight years of experience in the game of golf, forty-eight years of learning to appreciate the game and the venues at which it is played. A real appreciation for the game and the courses can never develop over a short period of time. One must experience the game before the golf gods begin to bestow a small knowledge of its true mysteries.

All of my travel has been in a motor home. We are, in the lingo of the motor home world, "full-timers." The motor home is our residence, a house on wheels ready to go almost instantly, and conversely, ready to stop whenever a golf course is spotted. This lifestyle quite naturally lends itself to the production of a book of this sort, if you're a golfer. In the process of doing a portion of the research, we traveled almost 9,000 miles across this great country during one six-month period and visited thirty-one of the United States, as well as Mexico. We went where the wind took us (which maybe wasn't such a good idea since we always seemed to be driving into a headwind). When we got tired of driving for the day, usually after three or four hours at the most, we parked the motor home and inquired about the location of the nearest golf course if we had not spotted one already. Usually we did not know in advance whether there was one in the area. But only on rare occasions did we fail to find one close by. That spontaneity led to marvelous and productive surprises. It was a Lewis and Clark–like experience. We never fell short of uncovering one that did not have a captivating reason for being, a unique feature, or both. On only a couple of occasions did we preplan a stop in order to investigate and experience a course. But even in those cases we were off the beaten cart path. We always needed directions to get to the course.

The diversity of terrains across our country is reflected in the great variety of designs of the golf courses that can be found. High prairies and deserts, mountaintops and valleys, Louisiana lowlands and South Dakota pine forests all provide settings for one-of-a-kind golf courses. We played courses in the Arizona desert and the high prairies of Wyoming. We discovered gems on the New Jersey shore and on the windy plains of west Texas. We encountered great stories in the mountains of western Virginia and among the pines, palms, and oaks of Florida. The conclusion? There's more to great golf than you find in expensive magazines. You just have to dig a little deeper and open your mind a little wider.

On the other hand, the journalistic experience was at times laborious and painstaking. Trying to describe golf courses or particular holes is not an easy task. It's kind of like trying to describe the taste of a banana. There are only so many descriptive terms available for the task at hand. So we tried not to be too tedious in the description of the golf courses or any particular hole. We also elected not to include a stroke-by-stroke replay of our rounds. No one really cares—especially us. (Occasionally, the ball was in our pocket before we finished the hole anyway.) This was especially true on courses at which the scenery was the crucial part of the story. It's hard to hit the ball when you're constantly looking up to enjoy the vistas and take a photograph. What we did try to give you was a general description of each course, as well as a few of the noteworthy holes.

Additionally, we tried to provide interesting, entertaining, and inspiring information pertaining to the course's history, tradition, and features—and the personalities involved with it. Knowing a little bit about what makes a course special makes it that much more fun to play.

In describing the greens we have tried to keep it simple. Greens are of a certain size, shape, and contour. Concerning their size, we have chosen to classify them as *small, medium, large,* or *extra large,* sort of like the way you buy golf shirts at the pro shop. Concerning their contours, we have employed the terms *slope, undulation,* and *level.* And on only certain occasions have we characterized the shape of a green.

The photography in this book is self-generated. No professional photographers were hired, and no professional photographs were used or purchased. You should be able to get a feel for what each course has in store for you from the three or four pictures provided; the photographs reflect the flavor of the courses very nicely. They were selected from a myriad taken at each course. Typically, at an eighteen-hole course we would take about seventy-five pictures, and at a nine-hole layout, about forty. This provided an adequate selection from which to choose.

The photography was fun. Not only was it exciting deciding which pictures to take, but it was also a great learning process. We observed what worked in magazines and books and then tried to incorporate that into our own photography. But we did not try to copy their photography. We wanted the photos to reflect what we saw and felt at each course. Therefore, there are several pictures that are not of the golf course itself: the pictures portray another element of the makeup of the course instead. Following each round we would anxiously download the pictures into the computer. It was always interesting to discover which pictures turned out well and which ones were just okay. (Mind you, there are no bad pictures of golf courses.)

Except for two, none of the courses on these pages will be found in the "best of" listings in any of the major golf publications. None of these courses, with the possible exception of Gray Plantation in Lake Charles, Louisiana, aspires to hold state or national championships. What you will find is a casual atmosphere, with golfers walking the course, playing the game the way it was meant to be played. There will be few yardage markers and certainly no global positioning systems providing precise measurements to the hole. Just eyeball it and swing away. You might not even find rakes in the bunkers; just smooth out the footprints as best you can with your foot or club. But the good news is a few of the courses have no bunkers at all. Chances are there won't be any granite tee markers with a pretty picture of the hole and a few other etchings, either: look down the fairway and figure it out for yourself.

There was only one definitive criterion for the selection of the courses in this book. They had to be off the beaten cart path. Many we were lucky to find at all; a few we discovered at the suggestions of friends and fellow golfers. All can be found in towns where you might not expect to encounter any kind of golf course—or at the least, not a course with great charm. These are not courses you will discover if you travel from airport to airport. (All this just proves that you should bring your clubs wherever you go.

Remember: discovering golf courses is like eating a box of chocolates.) We played several wonderful courses and observed many others that did not make the cut. And although we did not establish a price ceiling of $25 in order to be included in the project, you can play any course in this book except one for $25 or less. Gray Plantation is $48 and that's *with* a golf cart. Each and every course happens to be a bargain.

So, why a book of this sort? It's twofold. First, we have tried to instill in you the same desire we have to search out these courses and experience their stories. Hopefully, you will begin anticipate the journey, you'll marvel at the courses and the scenery, you'll enjoy the people, and most of all, you'll treasure the experience. You'll need to take a don't-forget-to-smell-the-flowers approach. That's what such an odyssey is all about. Second, we want to inspire you to create your own *Off the Beaten Cart Path*–type list. This volume is by no means all-inclusive. Of the sixteen thousand courses in the United States, it is safe to estimate that well more than half fall into the category this book is devoted to. A conservative estimate would be ten thousand. That's ten thousand courses that are unique, inexpensive, and inaccessible by private jet. That's more than a lifetime of golf courses that are waiting to be discovered, waiting to have their stories discovered and told.

In the process of compiling this book, we experienced a sudden rain delay in Sonora, Texas. There we were—seven golfers with four golf carts huddled under a tin-roofed rain shelter in west Texas. One golf story led to another, and as we explained the project we had undertaken, one player was prompted to comment, "That's a wonderful idea. It would sure be nice to know where there's a golf course nearby when you're traveling." That's true enough, and this book certainly fits that niche. But there are thousands more golf courses just waiting to be discovered by the avid golfer. Go to it!

"In the Heartland"

Bear Creek Golf Course

FOREST CITY, IOWA

Tucked away in northern Iowa, 17 miles west of Interstate 35 and 40 miles south of Minnesota, is Forest City, a primarily agricultural community in America's heartland. There is one exception to this agronomical lifestyle—Winnebago Industries. Yes, that's *the* Winnebago, as in motor homes. Winnebago employs about 4,200 of the town's 4,000 residents. Yes, those two numbers are in the correct position. Obviously the math doesn't work out, and that's why Winnebago draws its employees from a 75-mile radius. As a result of its employment base, it has some influence on most things that happen in the town. That would also include golf.

You can find down-home golf, entwined with a gentle dose of mom-and-pop, on the back roads and off the interstates in all of the forty-eight contiguous states. There are a countless number of towns that have their own local courses—in many cases just a nine-hole track. The friendliness is genuine and the golf is fun. Forest City is true to this

A view of the eighth green beside the Winnebago River

statement with one exception: its local nine-holer has grown into an eighteen-holer—make that a nineteen-holer.

But this change occurred only recently. The origin of golf in Forest City dates back to the first half of the twentieth century. Between World War I and World War II a nine-hole course with sand greens and a crude attempt at fairways was constructed on the south side of town. It was called River Oaks. During World War II that course was ploughed under, and the land was used to raise crops for food in support of the war effort. Today the area is owned by Winnebago Industries and utilized as a rally park. In the early 1950s, a new nine-hole course was constructed closer to the center of town, just south of the former River Oaks and east of the Winnebago River. This new course was named Forest City Country Club and for the first few years of play on the new course the greens were also of the sand variety. Unfortunately, the name of the architect for the project has been lost or forgotten.

The course remained at nine holes until August 2003, when a second nine holes were opened. The design was provided by Tom Haugen of Minneapolis, Minnesota. It is no coincidence that Haugen is a native of Forest City. The new nine incorporate the meanderings of the Winnebago River, which comes into play on six of the holes. Play is also influenced on two of the holes by a small tributary that feeds into the Winnebago River. This tributary is Bear Creek, which now lends its name to the golf course. When the second nine were commissioned, the name of the course was changed from Forest City Country Club to Bear Creek Golf Course. Bear Creek is aptly named. Folklore has it that around the turn of the twentieth century one of Forest City's leading citizens, Mr. Clark, was walking through the woods along the creek located north of the current location of the course. He was attacked and mauled by a bear, nearly losing his life. Shortly thereafter, the creek became known as Bear Creek, and Clark received recognition by having a street named after him in the center of town.

In keeping with the bear theme and emphasizing the notable difference between the front and back nines, the two nines have been nicknamed the "Cub" and the "Grizzly," respectively. The course plays to a traditional par of 72, but in a nontraditional fashion. The par on the front is 34 with three par 3s and one par 5, while the back play to a par of 38, featuring three par 5s and one par 3. And there is one unusual twist: the back nine are actually the back ten. The inward half features an extra hole (termed a "temporary hole"); a 180-yard par 3 wedged in between holes fourteen and fifteen. The original thought for such a feature was to have the ability to close a hole on the front nine for improvement and still maintain an eighteen-hole course. However, in the spring of 2004, just ten months after opening the back nine, the area was flooded, and the eleventh hole became unplayable for the whole season. The temporary hole was put into play to keep the course at eighteen holes playing to a par of 71.

True to their names, the two nines are completely different in how they play. The front nine have a classic design from the mid-twentieth century, featuring moderate-length holes defined by narrow, tree-lined fairways and small, rolling greens that are crowned and sloped for drainage. In contrast, the back ten are a testament to modern design, with wide-open fairways and huge, undulating greens sometimes featuring as many as four levels. Not surprisingly, an enormous double green serves the tenth and seventeenth holes. This eclectic mix of architecture provides a unique and challenging golf experience. It keeps you on your toes.

Double green that serves number ten and number seventeen

The front nine, with their half-century-old design, play quite short, with a maximum length of 2,850 yards and a par of 34. Nevertheless, they are no pushover. All of the holes are tree lined, and tee shots require maximum precision. If you're fortunate

Looking back from the sixteenth green. There's trouble in many forms on this hole.

enough to find the fairway, your task is only half complete. All of the approach shots must find the small, sloping greens to have a putt for birdie. And on all of the greens you must be below the hole or a three putt is a definite possibility. Number eight, the only par 5 on the front, is short but doglegs slightly right and plays along the bank of the Winnebago River. A tee shot too far to the left finds trees or water. If you decide to go for the green in two, you must guard against going too far left, as the green sits just 20 yards from the river's edge.

The back side plays to a long 3,724 yards from the back tees but a manageable 2,818 from the forward. The back ten begin with a dogleg left par 4 that requires a tee shot over a small lake and through a narrow opening in the trees. The approach is to the double green and demands exact distance control to place your ball on the proper side of a hump that traverses the middle of the green.

The long par-5 sixteenth, 589 yards, presents a difficult decision on the second shot. Once again the Winnebago River comes into play, diagonally crossing the fairway at approximately 175 yards from the green. The river literally splits the hole in two. On the second shot there are two choices: play across the river to about 150 yards from the green, or continue straight and possibly have a shorter shot to the green if you don't hit it too long or slightly left. If you successfully negotiate the second shot, your work is still not done. The approach is to a huge, undulating, humpbacked green that can easily throw a shot offline. Any shot not within 20 feet is in danger of a three putt. The hole requires nerves of steel just to make par.

Bear Creek Golf Course is entertaining and educational to play because of the diversity of its architecture. You must be extremely straight off the tee on the front and very long on the back. In other words, switch gears halfway through your round.

"I Did It My Way"

Belden Hill Golf Club

HARPURSVILLE, NEW YORK

Fifteen miles north of Binghamton, New York, and right on the old transport road now known as State Route 7 is Belden Hill Golf Club. Interstate 88 passes within a mile, but the course was here long before the highway. This is farm country, with hilly terrain and rocky soil. If the land were not a golf course, there would be cattle or crops occupying the space. This course has the fortunate distinction of being locally conceived, constructed, owned, and operated since its inception in 1947. It can surely be considered the epitome of the mom-and-pop golf course. Belden Hill owes its origin to Henry Fippen. In the 1940s, Fippen was an employee of IBM in Endicott, New York, and an avid golfer. He was also a member of the IBM-owned course on the outskirts of Endicott. When the

Opposite: Number ten is short, but straight uphill, and you must avoid the tree on the right.

The thirteenth and signature hole. While only about 100 yards, distance and direction are critical.

course raised its greens fee from fifty cents to seventy-five cents at the start of the 1947 golf season, Fippen became upset. He protested, but there was no room for discussion at the IBM course. So Fippen took matters into his own hands and produced a solution

"I Did It My Way"

to the problem. "The heck with you," he said, "I'll build my own course." And that's just what he did! Fippen found the land, designed a nine-hole course, and did a majority of the construction himself. The course opened for play in 1948. Ultimately, the course cost a whole lot more than a quarter per round, but Fippen was a man of principle. We benefit from his integrity and tenacity.

In 1952, Fippen handed over the ownership and operation of the course to his daughter and son-in-law, Frank and Beverly Burdine. They continued to upgrade the project, making a few improvements and alterations, but still keeping the course at nine holes. In 1972, the Burdines sold the course to local residents and club members, Mr. and Mrs. Newby. But the Burdines did not leave without a lasting memorial. When they passed away within a few years, they expressed their love for the course by having their ashes scattered over the first and ninth holes.

In 1995, the Newbys sold the course to Mr. and Mrs. Grady Whitenburg. The Whitenburgs realized its potential and in 1996, with the golf boom in full swing, decided to add another nine holes. They purchased a plot of land adjacent to the course. The terrain was similar, but a bit more wooded; it also contained small shale quarry. That quarry has been used most creatively in the design, and today it surrounds Belden Hill's signature hole, the 107-yard, par-3 thirteenth. The new nine opened for play in 1998, giving the course a full eighteen holes and playing to a par of 70, 36 on the front and 34 on the back.

The course is not long by modern standards, playing to 5,592 yards from the back tees and 4,234 yards from the forward tees. But the actual playing length is deceptive. Constant changes in elevation, especially on the back nine, add considerable length. On the first and tenth holes players must drive over a deep valley and hit blind uphill second shots to elevated greens. Both holes play much longer than the 248 yards and 313 yards declared on the scorecard. If you plan on driving either green you'll have to carry the ball the full length of the hole.

After climbing the steep hill to the first green, the front nine continue over a plateau with par 4s and par 5s until the eighth. The front side ends in an unusual fashion, with two consecutive par 3s, the ninth being a tricky downhill 207-yarder. It's a pleasant nine holes, giving you every opportunity to score well. And make sure you do before teeing off on number ten.

Despite being about 400 yards shorter than the front nine, the back nine provide the teeth of the course. The inward half, playing to a par of just 34, is hillier, narrower, and much more visually deceptive. All but two of the holes, the par-3 eleventh and the par-4 fourteenth, are tree lined, and there are obvious and subtle elevation changes on five of the holes. The signature hole is the thirteenth, a 107-yard par 3 that plays slightly downhill. The entire hole was cut from a shale quarry. The only grass to be found on the hole is on the tee, the green, and the fringe. An errant shot will ricochet wildly off the shale sidewalls.

Just two holes later is the par-3 fifteenth, which measures just 118 yards. The hole plays slightly uphill to a green that is long and narrow. At approximately 110 feet from

Looking back from the fifteenth green. Selecting the right club to play to the long, narrow green is a must.

front to back, it requires a one- or two-club adjustment, depending on the hole location. And don't miss the green to the right. It falls off sharply into the deep woods.

The final three holes will guide you uphill, downhill, and back uphill to the eighteenth green. These holes require precision and an accurate eye for distance. And the

The par-5 sixteenth is uphill all the way. It's a tough walk toward the end of your round.

sixteenth, the only par 5 on the back, will certainly test your stamina. It's 540 yards long and uphill all the way. In fact, from the tee box, you won't be able to see the flagstick. Just hit two good shots and you might be within 100 yards of the green.

"I Did It My Way"

The key to playing Belden Hill is not length but rather the ability to manage difficult lies. Throughout an eighteen-hole round, you will play from a variety of uphill, down-hill, and side-hill lies. How you manage your accuracy from tricky lies will determine your score.

And when you have finished your round, the kitchen and the pub are open. It's good home cookin' and of course, your favorite post-round beverage. And without a doubt, there'll be someone around to help you commiserate.

"The Raceway"

Canyon Breeze Golf Course

BEAVER, UTAH

"Eureka! We have found it!" Perhaps the words of the early pioneers as they made their way across the western part of our country, but definitely our words when we discovered a most unique golf course tucked away in a canyonlike setting in south central Utah. If we can define unique as simply highly unusual, then we have a perfect description of Canyon Breeze Golf Course in Beaver, Utah. The small town of Beaver, with a population of 2,500, does have a definite claim to fame. It is the birthplace of both Philo T. Farnsworth, the inventor of the television, and the notorious outlaw Butch Cassidy. However, it is probably not the kind of locale you would go to in search of a golf course—and a most unconventional one at that. But if you don't take the

Opposite: Half of the infield of the racetrack is the practice area; the other half is the seventh hole.

The site of the golf course has a rich history.

DAUGHTERS OF UTAH PIONEERS

No. 327
ERECTED 1966

FORT CAMERON - MURDOCK ACADEMY

IN 1872-73 A TWO AND TWO-THIRDS MILE SQUARE, PROTECTIVE MILITARY RESERVATION WAS ESTABLISHED FOLLOWING THE REQUEST OF C. M. HAWLEY, ASSOCIATE JUSTICE, UTAH TERRITORY. BUILT OF NATIVE ROCK AND LUMBER, IT RECEIVED 250 TROOPS SEPT. 7, 1873. MAJOR JOHN B. WILKINS, COMMANDER. FORT ABANDONED MAY 1883. L.D.S. CHURCH PURCHASED ONE-HALF J.R. MURDOCK, P.T. FARNSWORTH GAVE THE OTHER HALF AS A SITE FOR THE B.Y.U. BEAVER BRANCH. MURDOCK ACADEMY OPENED SEPT. 26, 1898. CLOSED 1922.

BEAVER CITY CAMPS

opportunity, you'll miss playing a course that is laid out, around, and through a horse track. There's even a hole that's routed straight through its infield: the seventh hole, the only par 5 on the course, plays at 500 yards, with the first 350 yards located on the infield of the racetrack. And that's only half of the infield: the other half is occupied by

The par-3 second presents a small target.

the practice area, where you can bring your own shag balls and practice in a stadium-like atmosphere.

So, what led to such an unconventional design? The racetrack was built in the late 1940s, but by the late 1950s the Lions Club of Beaver decided that the area around the racetrack needed some beautification. The idea that prevailed was a golf course, and in 1960, the club proposed to the city that they join forces to construct a nine-hole layout with the racetrack as its focal point. The city agreed, and the project was completed in 1961. The course was not designed by a well-known architect; it was handled by a committee of Lions Club members. Fortunately, they had some golfing experience and an abundance of creativity.

Canyon Breeze is also laid out around the site of Fort Cameron, a preserved military reservation that was utilized between 1873 and 1883. As you enter the parking lot, a stone monument with a plaque provides a bit of historical information. Additionally, Canyon Breeze has the distinction of being the first course constructed south of Provo, approximately 150 miles to the north. In keeping with its location, Canyon Breeze is the home of the Southern Utah State Amateur, a major Utah tournament that annually provides exciting and spirited competition. The eighteen-hole course record of 60 was shot during the 1999 championship by Larry Williams, who eventually won the title.

The nine-hole layout is composed of three par 3s, five par 4s, and one par 5, playing to a total par of 34. All of the par 3s are demanding, with the shortest playing to 181 yards. At 191 yards, number two is the most dramatic, featuring a downhill tee shot with a drop of about 50 feet. Although the green is small there are two levels, so it demands accuracy and expert distance control. Numbers four and five, the two remaining par 3s, play at 196 and 217 yards, respectively, and run parallel. You will always have the wind at you back on one and against you on the other.

These two signs provide all of the info you need as you head to the seventh tee.

The centerpiece of the layout is the racetrack with the par-5 seventh, going through the left half of its infield. As you leave the sixth green and head to the seventh tee, a sign warns you to watch for horses, noting that they have the right of way. There is no tunnel. You must cross over the track to get to the seventh tee. Caution is the key here. So

The ninth is a short par 4, but requires precision course management.

what happens if you hit an errant shot and your ball finishes on the racetrack? No worries—it's just a stroke penalty. A local rule on the scorecard explains that the "entire running area of the racetrack is to be played as a lateral water hazard." And on the few days a year when races are held, the hole is converted into a par 3 playing to about 150 yards.

The ninth is the best par 4, providing an excellent chance for a birdie, but not without considerable risk. The hole measures a mere 322 yards. Long hitters can even have a go at the green. However, the tee shot must carry a small lake located less than 100 yards from the green. If you elect to play safe to the left of the lake, a precise shot is required to avoid being blocked by a large pine that guards the middle of the fairway.

Canyon Breeze is simply a delight to play. It is fun golf in a most uncommon setting and despite the fact that it's not long by modern standards, it presents a considerable challenge. Small greens, three meandering creeks, and two strategically located ponds require accuracy on every shot. And the best part: you'll always receive a warm welcome.

"*Little Course on the Prairie*"

Chamberlain Country Club

OAKOMA, SOUTH DAKOTA

Just a little more than 100 miles west of the girlhood home of Laura Ingalls Wilder (author of *Little House on the Prairie*), along Interstate 90 in South Dakota, is the "Little Golf Course on the Prairie"—Chamberlain Country Club. It is truly prairie golf. The course is actually located in Oakoma, four miles west of Chamberlain and just across the Missouri River. Chamberlain Country Club is a haven for golfers in the area—with the distinction of being the only course within 75 miles.

Construction on the current course began in 1954, and play began the following year. It was incorporated as Chamberlain Country Club in 1956. But this was not the original course in the area. The original local course was situated on American Island in the middle of the Missouri River. In the early 1950s, during the development of the Dwight D. Eisenhower Interstate Highway and Defense System, the Missouri River was dammed in two places to facilitate the highway project. American Island, which contained a number of recreation facilities, including the local golf course for the town of Chamberlain and the surrounding area, would be flooded. Under the agreement for the project, the Army Corps of Engineers was required to replace the facilities on the island. Local government officials had four possible sites from which to choose for the new golf course. They selected land on the west side of the river. Unfortunately, this location can create some confusion. The course, the Chamberlain Country Club, is actually located in the town of Oakoma, on the west side of the river; the town of Chamberlain is on the east side of the river. To further complicate the matter, the course is owned by Chamberlain, which is in Brule County, but the facility is located in Lynn County. Got that? The good news is that it is all in the same state.

Despite the distraction of the name, the location is perfect. The course sits in a narrow valley immediately to the north of Interstate 90. It is, somewhat surprisingly, relatively flat. And if you're fortunate, you'll have a gallery consisting of the cattle that regularly graze on the hillside to the north of the course providing you with "moos" and "boos" always appropriate to your shot.

This is the land of the Old West and, as one might expect from the location, there are many colorful characters who have patronized or currently frequent this course. There are few white-collar members. You're more likely to see blue jeans and cowboy boots than FootJoys and Tommy Bahama—more persimmon drivers than Callaway Big Berthas.

The par-3 seventh is a thread-the-needle shot. Good luck!

At opposite ends of this membership spectrum are Joe Scales and Coleman Caldwell. Scales, who recently passed away, was a longtime member of the club who captured the club championship four times during his tenure, the last being in 2001 at the age of sixty-five. He also made three holes-in-one at the course, one on number four and two

This is the farthest point from the club-house, and appropriately rustic facilities are provided.

on number seven. A commemorative bench has been placed on the seventh tee celebrating Scales's achievements, and there is a memorial tournament held every year in his honor. Coleman Caldwell is at the beginning of his golfing career. He is a nine-year-old

Native American who is regarded as the Tiger Woods of Chamberlain Country Club and even South Dakota itself. At the age of nine Caldwell has already recorded two holes-in-one and won several tournaments in his age group.

The current layout was designed by a local golfer, Eddie Miller, in conjunction with the Corps of Engineers. If Miller's goal was an enchanting track, he succeeded. Restricted by the topography, all of the holes run east to west or west to east. And you can always depend on playing with some wind whipping through the valley. On the day we played, a 15- to 20-mile-per-hour breeze was blowing from the west, making the two par 5s, number one and number nine, play with the wind. Conversely, four of the par 4s played into the breeze, making them at least two clubs longer than their designated yardage. And to challenge your accuracy, American Crow Creek cuts through four of the holes and must be avoided on the tee shot. There is almost a total absence of bunkers: only two in the fairway and one that guards the first green. But this does not diminish the difficulty of the approach shots. On four holes the approach must be threaded through an opening in the trees to gain access to the green. There's room, but you can't have much push or pull on the shot. The greens are small, with a moderate amount of slope to provide for drainage, as well as to present the golfer with a challenge on downhill putts.

Golf is simple at Chamberlain, and there's no place for political correctness. There are two sets of tee markers. The scorecard designates the white markers as men's and the red markers as women's. There's nothing more; there's nothing less. And in keeping with the attitude and ambience of the course, if Mother Nature calls during your round, there are facilities on the sixth tee: an old-fashioned wooden outhouse.

The layout requires an interesting strategy. The par 5s are relatively easy; the par 4s are not long but require precise distance control; and the par 3s demand length and accuracy. The extremely short par-4 fifth is a good example. At its maximum the hole is only 265 yards, with a slight dogleg to the left. A couple of small trees guard the left side, but the hole can be driven. The only problem is a small pond located at the right front of the green. And the fairway tilts that way ever so slightly. The choice is yours: take the risk and possibly have a putt for an eagle (if you fail you'll make bogey on a simple hole), or play smart for a sure par, or maybe a birdie.

The par-3 seventh is the most difficult hole on the layout. One-hundred eighty yards from the white markers and 128 yards from the red, it plays slightly uphill to a very wide but shallow green that slopes from right to left. And the shot here would be simple were it not for two large trees that serve as sentries for the green. The first is on the left and sits 75 yards from the tee. The second is 20 yards from the right side of the green. Depending on the location of the hole, on any given day, you may be required to hit a draw or a fade to get close. And don't forget, the wind will always be blowing to make the shot even more demanding.

Is Chamberlain Country Club truly off the beaten cart path? You bet it is. With 75 miles to go in any direction before you can find another golf course, it certainly qualifies. Is Chamberlain Country Club worth the stop on a golf odyssey? You bet it is, especially if you want charm and hospitality.

"The Course of Dreams"

Garner Golf & Country Club

GARNER, IOWA

Long before Kevin Costner heard voices in the cornfields of Iowa telling him, "If you build it, they will come," the city fathers of Garner, Iowa, heard a similar call: "If you build it, they will play." This may be a bit of legend and not the definitive reason why the city fathers decided to build a golf course in the town of Garner in the mid-1970s, but the end result was a captivating nine-hole course that is fun to play, is easy to walk, and requires you to hit a number of quality golf shots.

Garner is a modest town in north-central Iowa about 15 miles west of Interstate 35. It's 12 miles from Clear Lake, home of the Surf Ballroom, the last concert venue of Buddy Holly and the Big Bopper. Yes, you can go there and have your picture taken on the site of music history. It's also 25 miles from Mason City, home of Meredith Wilson, the author

Opposite: Garner Golf & Country Club is charming, just plain charming.

and composer of the *Music Man*. Yes, you can go there and have your picture taken, too—at a shopping mall with a re-creation of the movie set. As for Garner itself, it is typical of many small- and medium-sized Midwestern towns, a close-knit community with its own nine-hole golf course that is to be enjoyed by all regardless of ability or social stature.

Each golf course has a distinctive origin, and Garner Golf & Country Club is no different. In 1974, the city fathers of Garner, hoping to revitalize the city's economy, realized they had to lure economic development, and investigated the possibility of developing a golf course. After several meetings and robust debate, they decided to move forward with the field-of-dreams theory. They purchased approximately 100 acres of a dairy farm on the east side of town and began the development of the golf course. The course opened on July 10, 1975. The dedication plaque from that day still hangs in the clubhouse. And the dream is being lived out today. The course is open to everyone and annually hosts a considerable number of corporate and local business outings that, of course, boost the local economy.

Typical of many local municipal and privately owned courses, there was no well-known architect for this project. Rather, it was designed by committee. But that fact did not prevent the creation of a golf course that is engaging to play. It's not terribly difficult for the average golfer, yet presents a challenge to a player with a high level of skill. That's what makes a golf course appeal to every golfer.

Garner Golf & Country Club plays to a par of 36 and can be stretched to over 3,400 yards from the back tees. It features a 585-yard par 5 that gently curves to the left and plays uphill the entire length of the hole. All of the greens are medium-sized with a

The fourth presents a daunting tee shot over a lake to a fairway that bends to the left.

moderate slope. There are three sets of tees: white and blue for the front nine and back nine, respectively, and red for whomever chooses to use them. The facility also includes a practice green with bunkers and a large driving range. To keep your game in shape, the upstairs of the clubhouse even maintains a golf simulator during the winter months.

The short par-3 seventh is seductive and can lure you into a double-bogey.

The actual layout of the course is somewhat unusual. It is circular, with the first three holes on the outside of the circle and holes four through seven turning to the inside. Holes eight and nine complete the circle on the outside, taking you back to the clubhouse.

"The Course of Dreams"

The most challenging hole is the par-4 fourth, which plays to a maximum length of 403 yards. Both the tee shot and approach will test your skill. The drive requires a precise shot over a pond and marsh area to a fairway that angles in from the right and seemingly does not exist. The hole tempts you to cut off as much of the angle as your nerves will allow. A slight draw is the best play here. But that's only half the challenge. The approach shot requires precision to avoid a lake that is situated to the left and rear of the green. And don't forget the tree line to the right. You'll need to keep the ball away from these menacing poplars.

The par-5 second provides just a touch of quirkiness. The hole plays straightaway until it doglegs 90 degrees to the right for the final 150 yards. The corner is guarded by a lake containing a pump house, at the top of which is a flag. A local rule on the scorecard states that all balls played to the right of the flag incur a one-stroke penalty, with the next shot being played from the drop area. This is primarily a safety issue, protecting players on the fourth green, but it gives pause to big hitters trying to reach the green in two.

The par-3 seventh perfectly exhibits the charm of Garner Golf & Country Club. Playing at 119 yards to a tabletop top green that slopes to the right front, the green is surrounded by water on three of its four sides. Any shot that misses to the left, or is short or long, will find the water. There is a bailout area to the right, but getting up and down requires a soft touch to the sloping green.

Fun and friendliness—that's what Garner Golf & Country Club is all about.

"Why I Love Golf"

Gator Landing Golf Club and Campground

HAWTHORNE, FLORIDA

Gator Landing Golf Club and Campground is why I love golf. Yes, there is a campground. In fact, about a dozen of the campsites are within 50 yards of the first tee and putting green. If you choose to stay there in an RV, you can watch everything that goes on. But the appeal here is the attitude. The facility is not pretentious in any way. No one requires that the greens be cut to a certain speed. In fact, no one really requires that the greens be cut every day. No one sees a pressing need that the fairway and rough be precisely defined since all of the holes have a tree-lined border. No one expects the pro shop

Opposite: The opening tee shot must be threaded through the oaks.
It's an easy par if you're straight off the tee.

to be attended at all times. If no one's there, just leave your money or pay up when you're finished. If honesty is part of the spirit of golf, and the United States Golf Association claims that it is, then Gator Landing defines that spirit.

Even the scorecard gives a little insight into the casual atmosphere here. The local playing rules state, "Fivesomes not allowed Saturdays, Sundays, or holidays before noon. No sixsomes allowed at anytime." Gator Landing has increased the traditional number of players in a group by one. But the real point is, no one much cares.

Located in north central Florida about a mile east of Highway 301, right in the middle of farm country, Gator Landing Golf Club opened in 1968. An investment group of seven golfers built the course, pro shop, and swimming pool. They commissioned it as Hawthorne Country Club. But by 1972, the project was bankrupt and the course had been abandoned. In 1980, a second investment group attempted to resurrect the course with a plan to build condos around the layout. That project never got off the ground, and the course was left to unrestricted growth until 1996, when Jerry Marcum purchased the course and began a campground on land adjacent to the property. In 1997, Marcum turned the operation of the course over to Paul Metivier, who is still the proprietor today.

The original 1968 layout still exists and plays to a par of 37, which includes three par 5s, two of which dogleg left through narrow rows of oak trees. The two par 3s can both stretch to over 200 yards. The fourth is 213 yards and finishes within 50 yards of Little Orange Lake, which borders the course on the east. All of the par 4s are short and offer

A few palm trees, right in the middle of the fairway, must be negotiated on the short par-4 eighth.

great birdie opportunities if you negotiate them correctly. Accuracy is the biggest challenge at Gator Landing. From the opening tee shot you're faced with fairways lined with oaks and pines. Despite being only 350 yards, your drive must be threaded through a narrow, 40-yard opening of oaks. Any shot off line will rattle around in the trees. If you find the fairway, you'll have a short iron to the small green and a chance at a possible birdie.

The 330-yard eighth hole is an intriguing par 4 requiring a strategic approach. In addition to being lined with pines and oaks, the hole has three palm trees that guard the right side of the fairway just 75 yards from the green. You must decide whether to lay up on the left side or try to drive the ball past the palms. A poor decision will require a tricky approach shot, but proper execution could lead to a possible birdie.

A couple of anecdotes will help give you a true feel for the ambience and spirit of this course. Because of its setting, wildlife is abundant on and around the golf course. If you pay attention during your round, you might see deer, wild turkeys, a local eagle, otters, and, of course, a gator or two. But unexpected members of the animal kingdom have occasionally wandered onto the course. In the not too distant past several head of cattle were spotted wandering the course in the middle of the day, displaced from a ranch a couple of miles away. The owner and several members jumped into golf carts and tried to round them up. As they started to gain control of the herd, the lead cow made a sudden turn and headed back onto the course right in front of the eighth green and behind the ninth tee. All the activity finally caught the attention of a local patron, who was moved to comment, "That's why we love Gator Landing: golf and a rodeo for five bucks."

One of the rounds we played here produced one of golf's more interesting comments in relation to the identification of one's ball. It was not the traditional or customary terminology we might be used to. However, it did prove to be appropriate and effective. As we walked up the ninth fairway to hit our approach shots, a family consisting of a mom, a dad, their son, and his wife was just heading down the first hole, which runs almost parallel, separated by 20 yards of oak trees. Their tee shots had squirted off to the right of the first tee barely 50 yards and landed underneath the oak trees. As they raked through the oak leaves in an attempt to find their balls, we heard the mother exclaim, "Did you find Dad's ball yet?" To which the daughter innocently replied, "What color is it?" And so we have a new method of identifying one's golf ball.

Gator Landing is one of those courses that invite you to take on its challenges. But you can check your golf snobbery at the door. There's no room for pretensions or presumptions here. A couple of the fairways are too narrow, and the greens are never fast. You may not find a PGA Tour superstar here, but you may find a future PGA Tour superstar just learning the game with his dad. It's a great place to learn the game. That's why Gator Landing is always worth the stop. And that's why I love golf.

" Golf Magazine Presents...."

Gray Plantation

LAKE CHARLES, LOUISIANA

In our ongoing quest for golf courses that were truly off the beaten cart path, it was not often that we followed the lead or acquiesced to the suggestion of a major golf publication. Their rankings of golf courses are highly subjective and consequently open to debate. Nonetheless, in September 2004, *Golf Magazine* produced a list of courses entitled "The Thrifty Fifty," a compilation of fifty courses that you can play for $50 or less.

On this list, at position number three, is Gray Plantation, located in Lake Charles, Louisiana. And even though Lake Charles is serviced by Interstate 10 and the Interstate 210 loop, this course is off the beaten cart path. Unless you travel with a golf global positioning system in your pocket, you'll probably have to ask directions to locate it. But the pleasure of playing this course is well worth the effort of asking. *Golf Magazine* definitely got its evaluation completely accurate in this case.

Confirming the quality of this course's layout and conditioning, it has already developed a reputation for top competition and is quickly developing a rich tournament history at the state and national levels. In 2003, Gray Plantation hosted the Louisiana Senior Amateur and followed that with the 2004 Louisiana Mid-Amateur. And in 2005, the Senior Amateur returned. In 2003 and again in 2004, the Tight Lies Tour, a mini-tour for prospective Ladies Professional Golf Association players, held its championship at Gray Plantation.

As a further testament to the excellence of the course, Gray Plantation has already received awards for its layout and conditioning. In 2001 and 2003, it was voted the number two course in the state of Louisiana. In addition to the accolades from *Golf Magazine*, *Golf Digest* voted Gray Plantation one of the top ten bargain places to play.

The course has a modern design, with wide fairways and large, undulating greens, many of which have two or three levels. Ninety-four fairway and greenside bunkers are strategically placed throughout the course, and 60 acres of lakes influence play on twelve holes. What's interesting is that the three shortest par 4s, numbers five, eleven, and sixteen, present the player with options. Taking a chance with the tee shot could lead to a birdie or even an eagle, but it could also result in a double bogey.

Architect Rocky Roquemore starts you out gently on the first three holes with a par 5 and two par 4s. All have wide landing areas and generous greens. By the fifth, a short dogleg left par 4 at 378 yards, the holes begin to require a higher quality of shot-making. Here you have the option of cutting the dogleg by driving over several bunkers or taking the

Scenic and deadly. The par-3 sixth sits right beside Prien Lake. It's all carry to the green.

safe but longer route. The sixth is a visually spectacular, 150-yard par 3 that plays over an inlet of Prien Lake to a green that slopes sharply from back to front. It's imperative that your tee shot be placed below the hole. The par-5 seventh, with its double dogleg, provides a course-management situation for every level of player. The challenge begins on

The eleventh is a par 4 that offers options. Playing safe is a good way to make an easy par.

the tee shot to a serpentine fairway. On the second shot a decision must be made. Long hitters may want to challenge the green in two, while short and accurate players can lay up to the right before hitting their approach over the marsh to the green. The trick is to choose the right strategy and not be adversely influenced by the temptation of an eagle or a birdie.

The tee shot at the sixteenth gives you a challenge. How much do you bite off?

Number eleven is a short but strategic par 4. At 370 yards it would seem to be a manageable hole were it not for the stream that lines the right side of the tee box and the fairway, then cuts directly in front of the green as the hole doglegs right. The shortest route is over the stream directly at the green. Long hitters may be tempted to give it

A view toward the seventeenth green with the stately clubhouse in the background

a go for a chance at an eagle or birdie, but the best play is straight down the middle and then a short iron over the stream and onto the green. It makes for an easy par and a possible birdie.

At number sixteen you're presented with a cape hole design: the hole curves sharply around a lake to the right. Depending on your courage, you can bite off as much of the hole as you like. The braver and more successful you are, the easier the approach shot will be to the large, severely sloping green. But you must watch your distance off the tee. A shot that goes through the fairway might find one of five bunkers that frame the fairway.

Gray Plantation is a mesmerizing course. It lulls you into a false sense of security because of its wide-open appearance. It does not give the impression that it is difficult. That is a wrong first impression. While your tee shot may find the fairway, the approach shot must be placed properly on the green to avoid a three putt—or worse. And there are a few holes that beckon you to gamble for a birdie, but failure will end in a double bogey. But most of all enjoy the surroundings: tall pines and cool breezes in an old plantation setting.

"For the Love of the Game"

Great Oaks Golf Course

MARIANNA, FLORIDA

Sometimes a name is just a perfect match for a golf course: Great Oaks is one such impeccable fit. Often names are strained, trying too hard to be catchy or cute. In the end they sound almost silly. Try names such as River Whatever, when the course is 20 miles from the nearest tributary, or Something Lakes, situated in an arid desert. They just don't seem apropos. A name for a golf course should be suitable and relevant.

Great Oaks Golf Course is just that; it conforms to its surroundings and tells you immediately what the course is all about. Its name brings to mind a course populated by aged oak trees on every hole. And that's exactly what you'll find there. On every hole, giant oaks protect the edges of the fairways and even serve as sentinels to guard the green on the par-5 third.

Opposite: This is why it's called Great Oaks!

Great Oaks is located in the Florida Panhandle on U.S. Highway 90, between Cotton-dale and Marianna. It's about 80 miles west of the capital city of Tallahassee. And while the second hole parallels Highway 90, you'll definitely need to drive slowly and look closely for the entry road, which runs 500 yards around part of the golf course to the club-house. A small practice range, the putting green, and the clubhouse itself sit on the high-est point in the middle of the property, with the course spreading out around them.

Great Oaks was created and is currently owned and operated by people who truly love the game. Originally designed and built by Floridian Richard Carrel, Great Oaks opened in 1990. Carrel owned and operated the course until 1998, when it was purchased by Matt and Brenda Hardoin of North Carolina. The Hardoins were former private busi-ness owners who began searching the Internet for a golf course to purchase about six months after selling their business. Why buy a golf course? "I did it solely for the love of the game," Matt Hardoin says. "I had been playing golf all my life and thought it would be fun to own and operate my own course." And yes, he did realize that owning and op-erating a golf course was a 24-7 job.

The Hardoins purchased the course and never looked back. Matt immediately set to work strengthening the quality of the layout by adding several bunkers and improving the condition of the course. Today Great Oaks is his own ongoing work of art, constantly being tended to and refined.

The appeal of Great Oaks is that there is great diversity in the layout: no two holes are exactly alike. For instance, holes four and seven are almost identical in length—

The opening tee shot requires great precision.

about 345 yards. But while number four is wide open with a fairly large green that slopes from back to front, the seventh is narrow—very narrow in the landing area—and requires an approach shot to a small green with a slope from back right to front left. There are a couple of holes that turn gently to the right and a couple that turn gently to

Giant oaks guard the direct line to the green on the par-5 third hole, but there is an opening to the right side.

the left. One par 3 plays slightly uphill, and one plays slightly downhill. Even though they are about the same length, club selection is totally different. If your distance control is good, you'll play from relatively flat lies. If it is not, you'll play all sorts of downhill, uphill, and side-hill lies.

"For the Love of the Game"

From the opening tee shot, every hole on this nine-hole gem will test your skill. Drives must be precise despite the sometimes wide-open appearance of the fairways. Any tee shot that is even slightly off line will be menaced by the oaks and pines that line the fairways. Approach shots to the small greens require exact distance control. All the greens have subtle slopes, and several have more than one level. The course has a par of 36 and measures over 3,200 yards from the back tees, but that yardage is deceptive. There are constant elevation changes. Only one hole can be considered essentially flat.

The opening hole demonstrates these points. The tee shot will test your nerve and shot-making ability. Played from an elevated tee just outside the clubhouse, this shot requires you to thread the shot in between a lake that encroaches on the serpentine fairway from the left and a fairway bunker on the right. The approach shot plays slightly uphill to a two-tiered elevated green that's guarded by a bunker on the front right. Selecting the correct club for the second shot is tricky. Par is a good score here.

The third hole is a gambler's delight. It's a short par 5 that measures just 480 yards with a slight turn to the right. But it has one unusual feature: two large oak trees guard the entrance to the green, one standing directly in front about 15 yards from the front edge. The brave will try to hit either a towering shot into the green or a low runner which, if it is fortunate enough to miss the trees, could set up a birdie or eagle. If you can't pull off one of those shots, you'll need to play to the right of the green and pitch on with your third. The cut of the fairway actually is to the right of the green, guiding you on a safer strategic route.

The approach to the ninth. With the proper tee shot you'll have a short iron to the green and a chance at birdie.

As you tee off on the final hole, be sure to enjoy the view over the lake and uphill to the clubhouse. It makes a wonderful setting for a final hole. But don't be intimidated by the lake. It really doesn't come into play if you can maneuver your ball down the right side of the fairway. From there the approach is a mid- or short iron to a medium-sized

"For the Love of the Game"

green that slopes moderately from back to front. The green is also guarded by bunkers on the left and right.

Great Oaks gives all of us a look into the spirit of the game. There is a love for the game itself, a love for the venue of the game, and a love for those who play the game.

"Movie Town"

Mountain View Golf Course

VAN HORN, TEXAS

Movie Town, U.S.A., and golf, too! No, this is not Hollywood, California. This is Van Horn, Texas. That's Texas as in west Texas, where the golf courses are few and far between. Along Interstate 10, Van Horn is 120 miles east of El Paso or, if you will, about 120 miles from anywhere.

While this may not be Hollywood, Van Horn has a volume of movie production that would make any small-town fairway green with envy. Because of its western landscape, location, and atmosphere, Van Horn lends itself to quick and easy adaptation for movie sets that involve the period from the 1850s to the 1950s. No fewer than three movies—

Opposite: American flags sit atop the flagsticks at Mountain View.

Lonesome Dove, *Dead Man's Walk*, and *Blue Sky*—have been filmed in the town and the surrounding area. And while we were passing through, a fourth, starring Tommy Lee Jones, who owns a ranch less than 20 miles away, was being shot.

If you need more to do, local restaurants offer several unique dining experiences— but only one houses a shrine. Chuy's Restaurant, in the center of town, is the home of John Madden's Haul of Fame. This football museum is a gallery of Madden's yearly pre–Super Bowl all-star team selections.

Van Horn is an unlikely location in which to find an intriguing golf course. Mountain View Golf Course is a strictly municipal course—no private country clubs here—that opened in 1972. It replaced a rather primitive layout with sand greens and sand fairways, which had been located on the opposite end of town near the airport. Prior to 1972, if a Van Horn golfer wanted to play golf on grass, he or she had to travel 120 miles to either El Paso or Fort Stockton. But the course may never have existed were it not for the generosity of a group of dedicated golfers. Each donated $100 or more so that construction on the course could begin. A plaque in the pro shop commemorates their philanthropic efforts.

The golf course is indeed rustic, but that is part of its charm. There is no well-appointed pro shop with neatly folded $100 golf shirts on display. But you might be able to find a bargain in the used-club barrel. There is no elegant dining room or lounge. But you may be able to get a cold drink out of the cooler. (Pack your own sandwich.) There

This plaque commemorates those responsible for the inception of Mountain View Golf Course.

are no showy yardage markers or global positioning system gizmos to give you precise yardage to the flagstick. But there are a few signs nailed to mesquite trees on almost every hole, providing the distance to the green. You won't find any stylish bunkers with

No fancy yardage markers. Just a few signs are nailed to the trees.

sod walls or railroad ties. As a matter of fact, you won't find any bunkers at all. And you won't get to warm up at a modern, high-tech practice facility. But you will get to stretch your muscles on a range with the appearance of a *Tin Cup* movie set. There is one concession to opulence, however, and it is more than appropriate. Each flag on all nine flag-sticks is a crisp, new American flag. They're not trying to make a statement or prove a point. That's just what they like here.

The allure is that Mountain View is just golf. That's all it was intended to be—and that's all it is. But you get much more than that. The town is set in a valley that provides 360 degrees of mountain vistas. And because of the high desert location, you'll get views of dust devils as they kick up the desert floor. That, of course, means you'll play your round in wind. After all, this is west Texas. On the day we played, we began the round with just a gentle breeze, but by the time we reached number four, the wind had increased to between 15 and 20 miles per hour. That, we were told, was a calm day.

Mountain View is a traditional par-36 golf course, which includes two par 5s and two par 3s. There are three sets of tees that can stretch the course to 3,341 yards from the back or play to a comfortable 2,417 yards from the front. It is friendly to players of all skill levels. The greens are small with moderate slopes, and are all slightly elevated, making the approach shots most intimidating when the wind is factored in. The par-3 third is the most captivating hole, and the most dangerous. It can stretch to 195 yards from the back tees and demands a carry over water to a green that is closely guarded on the left side by a large willow tree.

The seventh is Mountain View's version of a cape hole design. It is 382 yards and doglegs sharply to the left. While there's no water to carry as is typical with a cape hole,

The par-3 third requires a carry over water to slightly elevated green.

there is a small barranca that will swallow weak tee shots. A properly negotiated tee shot will leave just a short iron into the green. The two par 5s are excellent birdie opportunities; however, number nine requires the approach to carry over a small pond directly in front of the green and may require a layup before the approach.

But here's the best part: almost every hotel and RV park in town is a commercial member of Mountain View. When you stay at any of these facilities, your green fees are free. If you choose to walk (and the course is perfectly flat), you pay nothing if you stay at one of the participating businesses. The use of a golf cart costs a nominal fee. But playing Mountain View is never a nominal experience: it's real golf with genuine people.

"For Love of Country"

Rio Mimbres Golf Course

DEMING, NEW MEXICO

Deming, New Mexico, with a population of fifteen thousand, is immediately off Interstate 10. As you drive into the town, a series of RV parks line the right side of the road. Of course, a town that attracts this many snowbirds must have a Wal-Mart and some semblance of a golf course—at least a little nine-hole track for all the retirees to crowd onto during the winter months. The Wal-Mart is, in fact, just up the street from the RV parks, and virtually across the street is a golf course. And as it turns out, it's more than just a semblance of a golf course. It's a course that can trace its existence back nearly a century. It's a course that has a history of supporting the war effort during World War II. It's a course on which the greens will drive you batty unless you have a Ben Crenshaw–like feel in your hands.

Rio Mimbres Golf Course is located within the confines of the Chihuahuan Desert. It derives its name from the Rio Mimbres River. Like most other Chihuahuan Desert

The par-3 fifth leaves no margin for error on the tee shot, and the green slopes toward the water.

rivers, the Rio Mimbres (River of the Willows) is born high in the mountains, fed by winter snows and summer thunderstorms, and eventually flows out into the open desert. Situated in Luna County at an elevation of 4,335 feet and approximately 50 miles east of the Continental Divide, Deming was originally part of the Gadsden Purchase and later became the headquarters of the second transcontinental railroad, the Silver Spikes. Deming is a hidden gem of a town. The sun shines over three hundred days per year, producing dry summers and mild winters. The Florida Mountains to the south of the course serve as a backdrop.

Golf has been played on the site of the present layout for at least seventy-five years and probably closer to one hundred years. The exact date of the origin of golf in Deming is unknown. There are claims that it originated as early as 1916, yet others believe that it began in the early 1930s. While the precise date may never be known, it is more historic, and certainly more romantic, to endorse the earlier date. The original layout had sand greens and native grass fairways. It was raw golf, but it was still golf. In the early 1940s, the greens were converted from sand to magnetite to prevent the strong winds in Deming from blowing away the sand. The magnetite, which is heavier than sand, was mixed with drain oil to produce a stable and somewhat smooth putting surface.

No greater love hath any man than he who giveth up his golf course for the love of his country. When World War II arrived, the military elected to build an air base adjacent to and on a portion of the golf course. The airbase was used to train pilots for bombing runs, the clubhouse was converted into an officers' club, and the course closed for seven years. Hangars from the old airbase can still be seen on the south side of the course.

In 1950, the membership purchased the golf course from the city and converted the raw course to grass. The back nine were added in 1990 and the front nine rearranged at the same time; the par-3 ninth was converted into a practice hole. Today the golf course stands as an eighteen-hole, par-72 layout that can stretch to about 6,700 yards.

This yardage is not overwhelming, and the length of the course is somewhat diminished by the 4,400-foot altitude. But the course is not easily negotiated. One wonders just how this course can be so arduous considering it is so flat, fairly wide open, and somewhat lacking in bunkers—there are only eleven. The answer is found in two factors: the greens and the wind. All of the greens are large, with an abundance of undulation. As a matter of fact, it's hard to find a flat putt on many of the greens. And to make the challenge even greater, they are fast; not pro-tour fast or Augusta National fast, but fast enough to get your full attention on any putt that's not straight uphill. With difficult greens there is a necessity for all approach shots to be exact. The ball must find the right level of the green. Putting even more pressure on the approach shot is the absence of any major changes in elevation. This makes the course visually deceptive. And the wind always blowing through the desert only adds to the challenge.

The par 3s on the front nine are the most difficult holes on which to make par, and also the most eye-catching. The second is 226 yards from the back tees and plays slightly uphill. The large, sloping, elevated green is protected on the left by a yawning bunker. The fifth is a bit more challenging, with a much more nerve-wracking tee shot.

The approach into the par-5 fifteenth. You can go for the green in two but risk having your ball in a watery grave.

The maximum length is just 180 yards, but a lake protects the entire left side of the green, and the green slopes gently to the lake. Any tee shot heading to the left is in danger of getting wet. The tee shot must also carry over a natural desert area. And to

Hangars remaining from the WWII airbase can still be seen on the south side of the golf course.

add one more element of difficulty, the breeze always seems to be blowing right to left on this hole.

The back nine are a steady nine holes of golf, providing a combination of long and short holes. The two par 5s, numbers ten and fifteen, play 570 yards and 499 yards, respectively, presenting a nice diversity. One you might reach in two, and the other requires your choice of strategy. The fifteenth is a marvelous hole for a gambler. Although it's a short par 5 and tempts you to go for the green in two, the green undulates severely and is guarded in front by a lake. The only opening is on its left side. And don't forget to pay homage to the John Stewart tree on the fifteenth tee. Legend has it that it's the only tree he never hit.

Rio Mimbres is a course that has it all: an engaging history, a link to the history of our country, and a golf course that is challenging to players of all levels. The bottom line—bring your best short game and you'll score well.

ROCHELLE RANCH

4
323
353
360
393
444
PAR 4
HCP 1

"The Gift"

Rochelle Ranch Golf Course

RAWLINS, WYOMING

In the never-ending search for the spirit of golf and courses that exude that spirit, there are times when the search finds you. There are locations in this great country where you would hardly expect to find unparalleled and spectacular golf with an essence to match. Such is the case of Rochelle Ranch Golf Course in Rawlins, Wyoming. Never in your wildest dreams would you suspect that Rawlins, Wyoming, with a population of ten thousand, would be the locale for one of the finest courses you might ever play. Why would anyone want to build an exceptional golf course in a town located on the high plateau of Wyoming? Situated 150 miles west of Cheyenne and about 300 miles east of Salt Lake City, Utah, Rawlins is not a town in which you would expect to encounter a masterpiece.

Opposite: The hole marker at number four. Don't go for the green!

It was these thoughts that were on our mind as we traveled west on Interstate 80 toward Rawlins. In fact, the conversation went something like this:

Author *(with tongue somewhat in cheek):* "Well, what kind of golf course do you think we'll find in Rawlins?"

Photographer *(with apprehension):* "You never know. Maybe none!"

Oh, we of little faith. What a surprise awaited us!

As we approached the first exit for the town, we glanced to our right and gazed upon eighteen holes of golf literally carved out of the earth, each one moving in a different direction, chiseled separately out of the barren-looking landscape. Jaws dropped, and broad smiles ensued. We rushed directly to the course. What could this be?

The course, it turns out, was in its first full day of operation, the ultimate gift from Curt and Marian Rochelle (hence the name). Curt is a local sheep rancher and founder of the Rochelle Livestock Company who became financially successful through uranium mining and high-tech investments. Rochelle is also a philanthropist who remembers his roots. In the past he had donated several million dollars to his alma mater, the University of Wyoming. But Rochelle Ranch may be his most generous endowment ever. In 1999, Rochelle met with his lawyer and requested that a committee be formed in Rawlins to ascertain what Rochelle could do for the city. Almost immediately the committee determined that a golf course would be appropriate. The closest course was a nine-hole layout located 15 miles away in the petroleum-producing town of Sinclair. Rochelle agreed, and the wheels were set in motion. The project became a joint venture,

The fairway bunkers have an unkempt look and snag balls like Velcro.

with the majority of the financing provided by the Rochelles. The city purchased the land and the golf carts, and Rochelle paid for the design and construction of the golf course and the clubhouse.

The par-3 sixteenth plays over an area of scrub brush and sand with the green sitting directly against a large lake.

The major obstacle was the land—land that was simply not suited for growing grass. Rawlins is situated on an elevated alkali flat at an altitude of 6,800 feet. Agronomists felt the challenge of growing grass in such soil was insurmountable. But not the citizens of Rawlins.

"The Gift"

Enter Arizona-based architect Ken Kavanaugh. Kavanaugh may not be well known in the East (most his work is found in the West and Southwest), but he is one of a handful of modern architects who has a total hands-on approach to the whole process of golf course construction. With the challenge at hand, Kavanaugh began work. Five years later the course opened for play.

Although the course appears quite flat from Interstate 80, which passes to the south, it is deceptively hilly. It is not too difficult to walk, but you should be in decent shape. The layout is a masterpiece of design, with only two holes running parallel to one another. The remaining sixteen holes zigzag throughout the rugged terrain, making maximum use of the elevation changes—and elevation changes there definitely are. The fairways are generous and incorporate an interesting design feature: fairway bunkers positioned in the center of the fairways, forcing play to the right or left of the hazard. This feature is included on eight of the holes. There is virtually no rough in the traditional sense; only a thin 6-foot strip rings each fairway. Balls hit off the fairway find thick sagebrush, scrub bushes, and sand. Strategically placed throughout the layout are 104 sand bunkers.

Each of the four par 3s present a different challenge, with the sixteenth being the most visually deceptive. The hole plays to a maximum length of 250 yards, with the green positioned against the lake to its left. The tee shot must carry almost the entire length of the hole over a waste area of sand and scrub brush. Thankfully, there is a bailout area to the right, meaning a chance at par is most difficult.

Rochelle Ranch is a gargantuan golf course. Yardages vary from a massive 7,925 to a very manageable 5,706; however, five sets of tees allow players of any skill level to choose the challenge they feel is appropriate. Each tee box has a Western theme with appropriate markers to match. From back to front there's "Horseshoe," "Antelope," "Coyote, "Spur," and "Brand."

Two holes distinctly demonstrate the changes in elevation. The fourth is a horseshoe-shaped par 4 with an elevated tee from which you can actually see the green, directly to the left of the tee across the lake. But unless you can carry your drive over 300 yards, even from the most forward tee, you're forced to play down to the fairway and then hit an iron to the green.

The change in elevation is most dramatic on number twelve, a spectacular par 4 that can stretch to a maximum of 515 yards. Yes, that's correct, a par 4 that plays at over 500 yards. The tee box sits approximately 100 feet above the fairway and provides a remarkable view of the hole. You can see everything right in front of you. The following hole is a par 5 that gently curves around a lake on the left, with the fairway pitched slightly from left to right. At 640 yards from the back tees, it is reported to be the longest hole in Wyoming.

To aid the golfer in club selection, all of the sprinkler heads are marked with yardages to the center of the green. One-hundred-fifty-yard markers are designated by small windmills. The scorecard provides the player with diagrams of the green, which are divided into six sections, each indicating the hole location for the day.

The par-4 twelfth plays at a maximum of 515 yards and drops significantly from the tee. Avoid the fairway bunker at all costs.

Rochelle Ranch Golf Course may be the best bargain in the United States for such high-quality golf. The most you'll pay is $22 for eighteen holes on weekends. Cart fees are $20 for 18 holes. Although it will test your physical stamina, you can walk any time. It is a must-play for golfers who find themselves off the beaten cart path.

"Down the Up River"

San Pedro Golf Course

BENSON, ARIZONA

Nestled in the high desert of Arizona, 40 miles east of Tucson and partially visible from Interstate 10, is San Pedro Golf Course. San Pedro is not an old course with a history replete with quirky characters and magical events. It opened on January 24, 2003. Rather, a number of other features and facts make its story entertaining and worthy of being included in a treatise that searches for the spirit of golf off the beaten cart path.

The exact location of San Pedro is the Arizona town of Benson, which has a population of five thousand and sits at an altitude of 4,400 feet. Arizona is rapidly developing a rich history in golf, with cities such as Tucson and Phoenix annually hosting several professional tour events. Benson is not one of those municipalities considered an Arizona golfing mecca, but you will find two courses in town. One is an executive course; the other is San Pedro. San Pedro is one of those facilities where you can find the

Opposite: The best tee shot at number three is straight away,
then carry the barranca with the approach shot.

true spirit of golf. The polite, courteous manner of the entire staff and their willingness to talk about the course and share their knowledge of it make you feel welcome. They make you want you to play and experience their golf course.

In a golf world in which the term *links golf course* has been used for virtually every course that has not been built in the mountains, one must be cautious when describing a layout that way. It is fair to say, however, that San Pedro Golf Course is definitely a links-style course. Despite being in the high desert of Arizona, the course gives you that feeling from the moment that you step onto the first tee. And when you view the layout diagram on the scorecard, you realize this really is a links-style course, at least in the sense that the ninth green does not sit snugly against the pro shop and the snack bar. Instead, the ninth green is the farthest point from the clubhouse. The first nine really do go out, and the second nine really do come in. San Pedro, which is built on the site of an old landfill, has another unique distinction. It is the only course located on the San Pedro River, which flows south to north. The river comes into play on four of the holes.

Before you begin play, be sure to read the entire scorecard rather than just glance at the diagram of the layout. Pay special attention to local rule number one: "DESERT RULE IS IN EFFECT: Play non-turf area as lateral water hazard. Proceed under Rule 26-1." This precise verbiage means that the entire golf course is surrounded by a lateral water hazard. Think of it, if you will, as a golf course on an island in the middle of the ocean. A mirage at this point would be nice. In the absence of a mirage, we advise you to stay out of the lateral hazard. It is desert, and there are creatures and critters that fear no man.

Looking back from the ninth green. The small pond challenges all approach shots.

The one word to describe San Pedro Golf Course is *playable*. In keeping with the links style, the landing areas are generous, but there are numerous fairway bunkers that demand attention on the tee shots. They are especially prevalent on dogleg holes guarding either the outside or inside of the fairway. The greens are medium to large in size and only occasionally protected by bunkers. It's easy to hit a green; it's difficult to make the putt.

The par-3 fifteenth has a surprising drop from the tee. Selecting the correct club is tricky.

Architect Mark Rathert has included five sets of tee markers. The black tees stretch the course to its maximum yardage, a healthy 7,313 yards that is diminished a little by the altitude. But you don't have to be a long hitter; the most forward tees (silver) play to a respectable 5,262 yards. There's a gentle blending of long and short holes to make the course interesting and enjoyable.

"Down the Up River"

Several holes will catch your eye and also get your attention when you play. The par-4 third is unique and tricky to describe. The hole plays 421 yards at its maximum length, but the fairway is divided by a 15-foot-deep barranca, creating a right-hand fairway and a left-hand fairway. The tee sits at the beginning of the one on the right, and the green can be found at the end of the one on the left. The ideal tee shot will be played straight-away, allowing the approach shot to carry the barranca. Only the bravest will try to save distance by carrying the barranca with the tee shot.

The ninth is a gambler's par 5. It is a straightaway hole except for the last 75 yards, where the green is tucked away behind a lake on the right. With a good drive you might have a go at the green on your second shot. Of course, a bad shot will dampen your ball and your spirits. If you have less courage, it's an easy layup and then a short pitch to the green.

The back nine feature a number of interesting holes, with the fifteenth being the most dramatic. It's a 204-yard par 3 with a tee box that sits approximately 75 feet above the green. The large green is shaped like an upside-down top hat and is protected on the right by a bunker. While the shot is not particularly difficult, picking the correct club is. It is extremely visually deceptive.

San Pedro Golf Course is literally an oasis of golf in the middle of the desert and provides an enjoyable round of golf. There are no houses, no condos, and no swimming pools. It tempts you to gamble for that elusive eagle and rewards you for a good shot. It also demands a feel for club selection. In short, it's great golf on a links-style course.

"Golf and Garden Tools"

Santa Rita Golf Club

CORONA, ARIZONA

As we pulled into the parking lot of the Santa Rita Golf Club in Corona, Arizona (no, this has nothing to do with the beer), about ten miles south of Tucson, I noticed a sign next to the building that obviously functions as the clubhouse. "Pro Shop and Tin Cup Lounge," it proclaims.

"Look at that, honey! They named the lounge after the movie!" I exclaimed to my wife with heightened anticipation. There had to be a unique story to this golf course.

Five minutes later we were standing in the pro shop discovering that there is a very good reason for the Tin Cup reference. The ninth hole of the Santa Rita Golf Club was "cast" in the movie *Tin Cup*. The hole was used for the scene in which Roy McAvoy, played by Kevin Costner, uses a rake, an army shovel, a hoe, and a baseball bat as golf

Opposite: This guy runs the golf course—or at least he thinks he does.

The Tin Cup *movie poster hangs memorably in the* Tin Cup *lounge.*

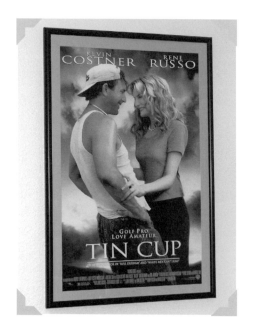

clubs to win a bet against a local fish. The scene occurs during the early part of the film. McAvoy, playing against one of his favorite betting opponents, wagers $400 that he can win a match using only the above-mentioned garden tools. Actually, he has no choice. His clubs are resting comfortably in a pawnshop, and he needs the money to retrieve

"Golf and Garden Tools"

them so he can attempt to qualify for the U.S. Open. In true Hollywood fashion, McAvoy wins the bet, gets his girl, and plays in the U.S. Open. The rest is cinematic history.

Do you remember that scene? Would you like to walk in the footsteps of Kevin Costner? Can you play a golf hole with a rake, an army shovel, a hoe, and a baseball bat? Well, this is the place to do it. Regardless of what you think of *Tin Cup* as a golf movie, you can play Santa Rita and re-create the Roy McAvoy experience—assuming, of course, that you have the proper equipment. But you will have to bring your own garden tools if you're going to give it a try. The pro shop does not rent tools, just golf clubs. And be sure to ask permission before you tee off with gardening implements.

While located close to Tucson, Santa Rita is unquestionably off the beaten cart path. With the multitude of courses in the area, you are not likely to seek out this jewel. It is out of the way. To get there, travel south from Tucson on Interstate 10, and take Exit 275 onto Houghton Road. Turn right (south), and go about 8 miles. Along this road you'll pass the county fairgrounds, several signs with pictures of cattle that say "Open Range" (another Costner movie, but with no relation to golf), and then come to a crossroads with a convenience store. Just past the convenience store on the left is the entrance to the golf course. It's so small you might miss it, so pay attention. But do find it. It's worth the stop, a lot of fun to play, and they're genuinely glad to have you there. In fact, we were invited to the weekly steak cookout. And make sure you take advantage of their outdoor patio. In the summer, water jets gently spray a cool mist on you after a hot round.

But Santa Rita is more than just a movie site. It's also an excellent golf course with some extremely difficult golf holes. Although it's fairly wide open, an errant shot will find the Arizona desert, a place you don't want to tread without a sand wedge in your hand. The greens are medium-sized. Many are just slightly raised, and all are well protected by bunkers, forcing all approach shots to be played precisely. There's no fooling around on this layout. You must be able to play golf in order to score well.

Like many of the eighteen-hole layouts that we have discovered, the two nines were built many years apart. At Santa Rita the front nine were constructed in the early 1960s, and the back nine opened in 1976. Actually, nine additional holes were added to the east of the existing nine and the order of play for the holes was rearranged, producing a somewhat unusual situation for golf courses in the United States; the ninth hole does not finish at the clubhouse. This reshuffling also generated another uncommon circumstance. With the course now at eighteen holes, par became 72, but with nines of 37 and 35 that include three par 5s on the front and three par 3s on the back. In total there are five par 5s and five par 3s, a bit of an unconventional mix of holes. The fun (and the challenge) of this design is that it provides both some good news and some bad news. The good news is that there is an abundance of opportunities for birdies on the par 5s. The bad news is that the par 3s are highly demanding, compelling you to hit the green or face a difficult up-and-down to save par. For ladies there is a bit more good news: the difficult par-3 twelfth becomes a par 4, making par on the back 36. The difficulty of the par 3s has even been acknowledged by *Tucson Citizen* Golf Editor Jack Rickard, who se-

The twelfth green sits as if on a tabletop and is guarded by two huge bunkers.

lected two of them for his "Toughest Eighteen Holes" in the area. Rickard ranks hole number twelve, playing at 220 yards, as the toughest, and number fourteen, at 195 yards, in the eighteenth spot.

A view toward the ninth green, the Tin Cup *hole.*

Santa Rita is also going to provide you with more than golf and a bit of cinematic history. You'll encounter an abundance of flora and fauna. After all, this is the Arizona desert. Don't be surprised to see more than a few roadrunners scampering across the fairways or staring you in the face as if to say, "How dare you invade my private playground with your little white ball!" And be sure to take your camera along to snap a few pictures of the flowering cacti.

If you're looking for a guaranteed challenge for your golf game, a chance to walk in the footsteps of a golf "legend," and to take in some of Mother Nature's amazing sights, Santa Rita Golf Club will provide it all.

"America the Beautiful"

Sky Mountain Golf Course

HURRICANE, UTAH

There are times when just the name of a golf course tantalizes us enough to search it out and tee it up. Sky Mountain Golf Course did just that, and the intrigue was further enhanced by the name of the town in which the course is located—Hurricane. How could you resist playing a course named Sky Mountain in a town called Hurricane (It's pronounced *HURR-i-kin*.) sounds like a sequel to *The Wizard of Oz*. The lure was just too compelling.

Hurricane is located in southwest Utah, a part of the state known as "color country." Indeed, colorful red sandstone ridges and jagged rock formations are everywhere. Black lava outcroppings surround the course, presenting an attention-grabbing contrast. If your senses are not overloaded after playing Sky Mountain, you can complete the visual feast by taking the 30-minute drive to Zion National Park, one of the most beautiful parks our country has to offer. In fact, do visit Zion National Park, and then

Every hole at Sky Mountain has been cut separately from the landscape.

play golf at Sky Mountain. You'll feel like you're playing a few holes right through the national park.

Sky Mountain was designed by Jeff Hardin and opened in 1996. It is owned by the city of Hurricane, making it a true municipal course. And while its age prohibits it from

"America the Beautiful"

having a long history, the real story of this course is its framework. If a golf course can partly measure its personality by its beauty, then Sky Mountain is in the running for Miss America. There are a fair number of golf courses with majestic vistas, and the competition is tough. But Sky Mountain still ranks at the top of the list. The scenery is almost beyond description. We could use highly evocative words—*astounding, striking, beautiful, magnificent, majestic*—but even these seem inadequate. On every hole, in virtually every direction, there is an awe-inspiring view. Once you get past the breathtaking landscape, you'll have a most challenging layout to play.

With a course rating and slope at 69.9 and 115, respectively, from the back tees, Sky Mountain is not a difficult golf course, if you are accurate. But it takes a Herculean effort to play golf at Sky Mountain. With its distractingly beautiful vistas, it's a demanding task just to concentrate on the shot at hand. A bit of advice: keep your head down, take your shot, and then enjoy the view. (And don't forget to watch for the abundant gallery of cottontails and jackrabbits, too.)

The layout is not long: just 6,383 yards from the back tees. But because of the exacting use of elevation changes from tee to green and the creative sculpting in the fairways, we found the yardage to be deceiving—some of the holes play considerably longer than you would expect and some play shorter, making club selection demanding and crucial.

When you play here, expect a stiff breeze. At Sky Mountain there is no such thing as a gentle zephyr. The town is named Hurricane for a very good reason. The report is that in the mid- to late 1860s, Erasmus Jones, a Mormon apostle and missionary, was exploring

The first hole plays downhill against a backdrop of mountains that appear to be a staircase to heaven.

the area. From a ridge overlooking the area, Jones had himself lowered down on a rope into the valley. During the exploration the high winds came up and tore apart his covered wagon, causing Jones to exclaim, "Feels like a hurricane!" The area became known as Hurricane Valley. When the town was incorporated in 1906, the name "Hurricane" stuck.

"America the Beautiful"

The tee shot to the eighth. Yes, it is possible to hit the green.

The front nine are the most scenic. The view from the first tee and the adjacent practice area present a striking panorama of mountaintops that look like a stairway to the sky. Now, after being visually distracted, you are required to hit your opening tee shot on this downhill par 4 that curves gently to the right. If you can hit a tee shot that is high

From the ninth tee you can walk straight up the mountains and into the clouds.

and curves slightly left to right, you'll enjoy the visual sensation of your ball soaring against the mountainous backdrop. From there you'll have just a short iron to a relatively open and flat green.

Play the seventeenth as it was designed: a drive to the corner of the dogleg and then the approach. There is no other way.

Holes four and five, both par 4s, are virtually identical in length and run parallel, but present contrasting problems. The fourth plays uphill to the green, making it longer than its 392 yards, while number five begins from an elevated tee, reducing the listed

The par-5 eighteenth can be a birdie hole if you don't get distracted by the view one last time.

yardage considerably. Standing on the eighth tee facing a 176-yard par 3 that plays over a pond, lava, and shrub brush to a tabletop green, you will think that a chance for a green in regulation is almost impossible. Fear not. A soft, high shot will give you a chance for par or a birdie. The tee on the par-5 ninth will once again fill your eyes with

"America the Beautiful"

a view of the heavens. As the hole curves gradually to the right, it seems to disappear into the sandstone rock formations.

The back nine roll gently until you reach the final two holes. Both of them appear to hang on the edge of a cliff. When you stand on the seventeenth tee, your visual meter will jump all the way into the red. The view is awe-inspiring, and the tee shot is nerve-wracking. Errant shots to the right are gone forever, lost in the abyss below. While the seventeenth is short (a maximum length of 388 yards), it is a 90-degree dogleg to the right. The tee shot must be played to the corner of the dogleg to allow for an open approach to the green. There is no cutting the corner, and any shot attempting to do so may never be found again.

When you arrive on the eighteenth tee, if you have a fear of heights, do not look to the right. The view is magnificent, but the drop is abrupt. The hole is a short par 5 of only 488 yards but requires a precise tee shot that curves slightly from right to left, and the fairway narrows as you close in on the green. And as you leave the eighteenth green, take one more moment to soak in the majestic view.

One final note on Sky Mountain: bring your camera.

How About Those Britches?

Original members of the Suwannee Country Club were: (l-r) Joe D. Radford, Frank D. Helvenston, Charlie Sherman, Dr. W.C. White, former governor Cary A. Hardee, Sidney A. Hinely, D.K. Clippinger, Reginald H. Helvenston, Henry E. Leech, J. Lynus Blackwell, Samuel E. Fleet, Henry Wynn, Edward S. Connor, Joe Hinely, Brantley W. Helvenston Jr., E.L. "Snake" Anderson and Claude J. Hackney. This photo is dated March 17, 1925 and was provided by Mrs. F.D. Helvenston.

"Old Man River"

Suwannee Country Club

LIVE OAK, FLORIDA

Located just a few miles from the musically historic Suwannee River is the like-named Suwannee Country Club. The course itself is a bit like "Old Man River" in that it dates back to the early 1920s. A picture of the seventeen original members dated March 17, 1925, hangs in the pro shop as a remembrance to their tenacity and love of the game. One of the members of the group was even a former governor of the state of Florida— Cary A. Hardee.

In fact, that this course still survives is a tribute to its members' resolve. The original layout still exists today, modified only to accommodate modern golfing technology. At its inception the greens were sand-based, treated with oil to provide for smooth putting. The condition of the course was rugged at best. As the quality of the grass improved, the

Opposite: The start of Suwannee. The photo is dated March 17, 1925.

Lou Mills dedication to Suwannee CC is demonstrated by a plaque in the clubhouse.

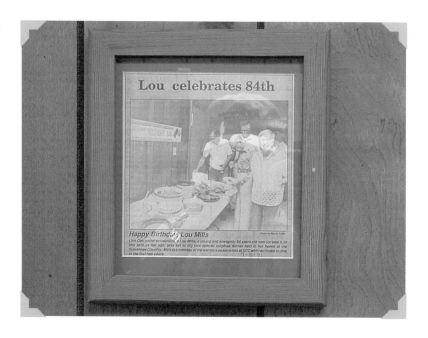

number of members increased, and the course thrived until World War II, when the amount of golf played dwindled to virtually nothing. Eventually, as part of the war effort, the course was turned into a pasture for cattle. Then in the early 1950s, the members began to restore the course by themselves, providing the funding and the labor. The sand greens endured until the late 1950s, when they were converted to grass. In 2000, the greens were redone, utilizing modern technological improvements. Today the course is still owned by the membership, which totals about 160.

Throughout the United States we have encountered many wonderful individuals who love the game of golf. They are not the marquee names of golf; they are not in the business of golf; they are not even accomplished players. They simply love the game just as much as the rich and famous. The Suwannee Country Club provided us with one of these marvelous human beings. While attempting to uncover the history of this splendid old course, we were given the name of Lou Mills. Ms. Mills was ninety-seven when we spoke with her, and she had been playing at Suwannee for almost fifty years. When the greens were converted to grass in the 1950s, it was Lou Mills who handmade the flags for the flagsticks. But Lou is more than just a dedicated member. She is also an accomplished player, with two holes-in-one on her golf resume, made in consecutive years at the ages of 83 and 84. And it was she who graciously provided the history we needed for the Suwannee Country Club. It was truly a memorable conversation with a lady who was entertaining and excited about sharing her experiences—she embodies the true spirit of golf.

Even at its longest, the Suwannee Country Club measures just less than 3,100 yards. But it is deceiving. Its tree-lined fairways demand accuracy, and it has surprising changes in elevation on all but three of the holes. The greens are small and tricky. All have either multiple levels or pronounced slopes for drainage. It is not an easy par of 36.

The arrangement of holes three and four, and holes twelve and thirteen, is also quite interesting if you play around twice to make eighteen holes. On the front nine, number three plays as a par 5, and number four as a par 4. On the back nine, the situation is reversed. It's a simple matter of tee box placement. This arrangement also forces you to change your strategy depending on the tee box you play. It all adds to the appeal of the golf course.

If you're hitting the tee ball accurately with moderate distance, you'll need only a short iron for the approach to all but one of the par 4s. But remember, the greens are small, and any shot missing the green leaves a difficult up-and-down for par. The second hole is a good example. It measures just 313 yards but plays over a small ravine and then uphill to the green for the final 150 yards. But the approach shot to the small, two-level green that is protected in the front by a long, narrow bunker shot must be precise. Not only is the distance deceiving for the second shot, but any ball missing the green is a difficult up-and-down.

The two par 3s are not long (135 and 165 yards, respectively), but require accurate tee shots and a steady putter. The fifth has a moderately sized green that rolls gently from back right to front left. Any tee shot that finishes above the hole is in danger of three putting. The eighth is straight uphill to the largest green on the golf course. But make sure you account for the breeze that may be coming off the lake to the right. Getting the correct distance here is tricky.

The second hole plays over a ravine and then uphill all the way.

On a charming golf course there is always one hole that displays charisma, a unique hole that has an anecdote behind it—perhaps part truth and part folklore. At Suwannee it is the finishing hole. At 330 yards it is quite short. But when you stand on the tee, you

The tale of "Garner's Gap" is commemorated with a plaque on the ninth tee.

GARNER'S GAP

J. GARNER CARMICHAEL
"DOC"
1933-2000

The 9th hole was Garner's favorite piece of real estate. He always had trouble getting to the green. So, one day Garner decided to fix that problem and brought the Florida Power and Light bucket truck and cut a gap in the trees going up the hill. From that day forward it has been known as Garner's gap.

Dedicated by family and friends
August 25, 2001

can't see the green. The hole doglegs 90 degrees to the right about 100 yards from the green. Then the approach is through a narrow gap in the tree line straight uphill to a green that slopes steeply from back to front. But this gap was not always there—not until J. Garner Carmichael, a longtime member, took it upon himself to borrow a Florida Power and Light bucket truck and do a bit of tree work on his own. To protect all of the parties involved, no date has ever been affixed to the deed. Henceforth it has been known as "Garner's Gap." A plaque sits on the ninth tee commemorating this auspicious deed.

It is the name. It is the history. It is the tradition that makes Suwannee Country Club a hidden gem that is off the beaten cart path.

"Après Ski"

Swiss Fairways Golf Course

CLERMONT, FLORIDA

A golf course *and* a Swiss ski school—what could be better? A sport for the summer and a sport for the winter. During my military career, I played on several golf courses in Europe, primarily in Germany and Austria, that also served as cross-country ski facilities in the winter. You can guess which sport has the longer season there.

To make this facility more engaging, the address of Swiss Fairways is Skiing Paradise Boulevard. So put the clubs in the trunk and the ski rack on the roof. But before you go, please check the exact location. Is this Breckenridge? No. Zurich? No. This is central Florida, U.S.A. So make sure you pack the right skis. This is a water-skiing school. (Did you really expect to find snow skiing just 30 miles from Orlando and the Mouse House?) This unusual golf course, right in the middle of Florida, will defy your expectations, too.

Opposite: The par-3 second is creative architecture at its best. There is no room for error on this hole.

We first discovered this golf course in 2001, tucked away in a small town in Lake County just to the northwest of Orlando. And it is a bit secluded. You'll have to look carefully for the wooden directional sign on Route 50 so you don't miss the turn. We liked Swiss Fairways then and we like it just as much now. It is no-frills golf on a superb layout in a most unusual setting. And did we mention the great bargain? It's right around $25 including cart during the prime season—in Florida! Admittedly, despite the no-frills approach, we originally thought that the double-wide trailer adapted for use as a clubhouse was just temporary. Surely there would be a more permanent building erected. But three years later when we returned, we found the same structure. It had survived three hurricanes during the summer of 2004. Now we realize it may be permanent. This is just an indication of the laid-back approach at Swiss Fairways. The parking lot is gravel, and you'll find a metal bag stand that serves as the bag drop next to the trailer. Place your clubs here when you go up the wooden ramp and into the trailer to check in.

In keeping with its basic, keep-it-simple theme, the course itself is rustic. The bunkers are usually unkempt; there's no precise edging here. And the rough is rough, usually left to grow as it may. This doesn't present a problem during the winter when the Bermuda grass is dormant, but in the summer it demands accuracy and tests your strength should you stray from the fairway. Don't expect not-a-blade-of-grass-out-of-place-type grooming, but do count on a distinctive layout with a diversity of long and short holes. There are holes that bend left and holes that bend right. And several holes

A sign warns you on the second tee which sport has priority.

boost your driving distance, and your ego, by allowing you to play from elevated tees. For short hitters these holes can be easy with an accurate tee shot. But the real work of art at Swiss Fairways is the seven holes that play either across or alongside the canals and small lake that serve as the ski school runs.

The twelfth is a short par-4 but tricky. It is drivable, but the approach requires great touch.

If every golf course must have a signature hole, then the second at Swiss Fairways is the consummate one. It is the obligation of a signature hole to define a golf course, and this spectacular par 3 accomplishes that perfectly. It is one of the most demanding, panoramic, and unusual par 3s that you will ever play. Depending on your choice of tee markers, the hole plays from 121 to 204 yards. (There is also an extreme forward tee playing to 80 yards.) The tee shot requires a carry over one of the training canals to a green that has been carved out of a hillside and is surrounded by bunkers and framed by tall pines in the back. A weak tee shot meets a watery grave, and an inaccurate one is severely punished with a difficult up-and-down. Double bogey is a common score—and sometimes a good score. And make sure you pay attention to the warning sign on the tee. Boats and skiers have the right of way.

As with many of the eighteen-hole courses we have uncovered on our travels, the two nines at Swiss Fairways were not constructed simultaneously. The front nine opened for play in 1989, and then in 1997, architect Steve Nugent was commissioned to create an additional nine holes. Nugent did a masterful job of blending the back nine and the front nine, creating the illusion that all eighteen holes were constructed at the same time. The flavor and charm of the front nine is faithfully re-created on the back.

If you're lacking confidence with your driver when you come to Swiss Fairways, then this course will help to restore your resolve. The wide-open fairways will make you tear off that head cover and give it a rip. To add further boldness to that drive, many of the fairways are mounded on the left and right, frequently providing friendly bounces. The real test is on the approach shots into the large, abruptly sloping greens. It is imperative to place your shot below the hole on the greens. If you fail, you'll get more use out of the putter than you would normally desire.

There's an adequate practice area with a driving range and putting green. Unfortunately, it's located well away from the clubhouse, making it a bit inconvenient to hit a few warm-up shots or practice putts before your round. It nevertheless provides the necessary requirements to prepare for your round.

For long hitters—the 300-yard plus-bombers—there are three par 4s that are possible to drive, but they do not come without a risk. The ninth is a 370-yard par 4 that doglegs 90 degrees to the right, making the hole considerably shorter if you choose the direct route from the tee. Failure to produce the perfect tee shot will lead to a double bogey or higher. A big blast from a long hitter might clear the tree that guards the right side of the green and present the player with an eagle putt. The twelfth is a short two-shot hole that will also tempt a big hitter. It measures a mere 340 yards from the back tees. This hole is another that plays directly across one of the ski run canals. There's nothing in the way on this hole, so give it a rip. The fourteenth is 10 yards shorter than the twelfth. The quandary here is that the hole doglegs 90 degrees to the right about 75 yards from the green, which is guarded on the left by a large pond. To drive the green you must carry the ball the full 330 yards. Even then you're not assured of a birdie. The green slopes sharply from back to front.

But don't be misled; the course is not short. There are four par 4s that play over 400 yards, and two par 5s, both on the back nine, which cover 600 yards each. The final hole will test your stamina after a demanding round. The 600-yard par 5 plays slightly uphill all the way as it bends gently to the left. Making par requires long and accurate shot-making.

Swiss Fairways is a singular golf experience. You'll delight in a layout with a wide variety of holes in a most unusual setting. Try Swiss; it's a must!

"*The Little Course That Could*"

The Pines

CLERMONT, NEW JERSEY

When some golfers hear the words *executive golf course*, their upper lips curl, their knees begin to buckle, and they throw away their drivers. Visions of Astroturf greens and rubber-mat tees dance in their heads. "That's just not for me. I prefer real golf," they mutter quietly as they turn away, trying not to outwardly exhibit the truth of their golfing arrogance.

Admittedly, many—no, make that most—executive golf courses have a tainted image in the golf world. They're a place to take the family when they want to "experience" golf. That means lots of kids, and clubs and balls flying everywhere. But a well-designed, well-maintained, short-yardage golf course can be fun and a test of one's golf game. This is especially true if the course has a mix of challenging par 3s and par 4s that

Opposite: A view over the putting green and down the first hole

require you to make critical decisions. The par 3s should demand a variety of clubs from the tee, and the par 4s should necessitate proper course management.

So let's go to The Pines, a nine-hole executive course located in the small southern New Jersey town of Clermont, not far from the beach towns of Ocean City and Wildwood. It's a course that more than meets all of these requirements and requires you to use every club in your bag. So bring all fourteen.

The Jersey Shore is a popular, well-known summer vacation destination. Families from all over New Jersey and eastern Pennsylvania flock to its beaches for a little summertime sun and fun. Also participating in this annual migration pattern are golfers. When Mom and the kids gather up the shovels, buckets, and sunscreen and head for the sand and the surf, Dad fires up the SUV and ventures to the nearest links. Fortunately, there's an abundance of golf courses. Unfortunately, during the summer season, they're all expensive, and the pace of play is just slightly faster than two snails in a drag race on the beach.

But there is a solution to this difficult, crowded, and expensive problem: The Pines. The Pines is a nine-hole course that presents a stiff challenge to players of every skill level. This is not your everyday par-3 golf course for which you need little more than a wedge and a putter to play your whole round. This golf course is downright imposing, featuring four par 4s and five par 3s for a par of 31. The par 4s vary in length from 273 to 403 yards, and the par 3s from 127 to 188 yards. The course was designed by its local

Each of the par 3s at the Bermuda Triangle requires a different club and shot.

owners, Mickey Gardner and Vince Orlando, yet the architecture is far from amateur. Each hole has distinctive shot values, and accuracy is at a premium. The four par 4s are laid out so that two require a left-to-right shot from the tee and two demand a right-to-left shot. A wayward tee shot will be swallowed by tall New Jersey pines. The course has a large putting green and practice bunker situated directly in front of the clubhouse, between the first tee and ninth green.

The five par 3s are all different and present the greatest challenge on the course. Each one calls for a different club from the tee and a different shot-making skill. The Pines even features its own miniversion of Amen Corner. Holes five, six, and seven form a neat triangle of demanding par 3s around a small lake that comes into play on each hole. They are affectionately known as the Bermuda Triangle. Number five plays to a maximum of 190 yards to an elevated green with three distinct levels. Number six stretches to 180 yards to a green that measures 135 feet from side to side. The green is guarded on the left side by a huge bunker. The seventh is 161 yards to a green that is guarded on the front and left by the lake. The only opening is to the right. The green slopes moderately from the top right to the lake on its left. Fortunately, there are two bunkers on the left side to snag any ball headed to a watery grave.

The eighth is a short par 4 that calls for a difficult decision. You may elect to try to drive the green, in which case you'll have to avoid four fairway pot bunkers on the right side of the fairway and thread the shot into a narrow, 10-yard opening at the front of the green. Or you may choose to lay up and have a wedge for your approach shot to a green that sits at a 45-degree angle and is protected on the left by a long, narrow bunker.

Here's the bottom line on this perfect executive course: bring your whole bag of clubs, a straight shot from the tee, and a good putting stroke for the fast, bent-grass greens. A couple of extra balls wouldn't be a bad idea either.

"Aces and Eights"

Tomahawk Country Club

DEADWOOD, SOUTH DAKOTA

Located just a few miles from the old Western gambling town of Deadwood, nestled snuggly in the pine forests of the Black Hills, is Tomahawk Country Club. This nine-hole course traces its origin back to 1934 and still maintains its original layout. It was created primarily to provide recreation for miners. Today it provides enjoyment to locals and tourists alike.

The historic town of Deadwood, with the ghost of Wild Bill Hickok in residence, makes this an interesting stop on any traveler's expedition. Nowadays Deadwood is a tourist center complete with gambling halls, saloons, museums, and souvenir shops. But don't be turned off by the possibility of tackiness. It's charming, the locals are friendly, and a good time can be had by all. The town should definitely be on your list of things

Opposite: The third has seen a multitude of aces, but is not an easy hole. But it is pleasing to the eye.

to do when you're not at the golf course. Mount Rushmore and a seemingly endless variety of other Black Hills attractions are also within easy driving distance. But don't forget the golf. There are plenty of golf courses in the Black Hills area.

We have designated Tomahawk as the hole-in-one, or "aces," course. Yes, this is in keeping with the gambling theme so prevalent in the history of Deadwood. (Legend has it that Wild Bill Hickok was shot holding a hand that contained aces and eights.) No, this is not coincidental. There have really been a large number of holes-in-one at Tomahawk. Inside the rustic clubhouse, which looks out over the eighteenth green and first tee, are numerous plaques testifying to them. While many courses pay homage to the patrons who experience golf's ultimate thrill, few do so as prominently. A quick investigation of these records reveals an impressive number of golfing milestones. The name of Connie Olson, a longtime member, appears three times in testament to her aces on the third. Betty Coburn has accomplished this feat twice at the same hole. And in a family affair, Al Varland, his son Rick, and daughter Tracy have all played the third in one stroke. Is the third easy? In fact, no! And neither is the other par 3, the eighth. It's just that these guys are good.

Tomahawk presents an unusual design and an entertaining challenge for the golfer. In just nine holes the terrain divides the golf course into two distinct sections. The course is set in a small valley, and the first five holes play over hilly terrain, providing marked changes in elevation for tee shots and approach shots. Then, after a 400-yard trek from the fifth green to the sixth tee, the final four holes play on relatively flat ground. Your shot-

The par-4 second is a dogleg right with a fairway that slopes to the left—a difficult tee shot.

making ability will be tested here as you try to maneuver your ball around a meandering stream that comes into play on each hole.

As with many older golf courses, it is accuracy and not length that is critical. Fortunately, the demand for the straight ball has been somewhat reduced in recent years

The long eighth requires a tee shot over a creek that cannot be seen from the tee.

with the removal of over 250 trees. The course demands another character trait: patience, especially on the first five holes. Downhill tee shots and uphill approaches to medium-sized undulating greens make club selection demanding and a well-rounded short game a necessity. The ultimate test in fortitude comes at the second, a 385-yard par

"Aces and Eights"

4 that doglegs right with a fairway that slopes hard to the left. To find the fairway here requires some exceptional golfing wizardry.

There are three sets of tees, accommodating all skill levels. From the back tees the length is 3,390 yards but plays considerably shorter at the 4,000-foot altitude. But don't be fooled by the extra distance you gain with the altitude. The first six holes all have changes in elevation either from the tee or on the approach shot, making club selection difficult.

The par-3 third hole is the most spectacular. At its longest it plays to 179 yards and drops 50 feet from tee to green. The two-tiered green slopes from right to left and is guarded on the left by a small bunker. The entire hole is surrounded by tall pines, leaving no room for error. Yes, this is the hole where an abundance of holes-in-one have been made, but it is no pushover. Missing the green will usually result in a bogey or worse.

The final three holes present a challenge of accuracy and length. The seventh is a 540-yard par 5 that is traversed by a creek, making the landing area smaller than it might appear. The approach is to an elevated green protected by pines on the left. The eighth is a par 3 that plays to a maximum length of 225 yards. The same creek snakes its way in front of the green just 25 yards from the putting surface, which is not visible from the tee. Finally the ninth, a 440-yard par 4, will require you to once again avoid the creek on your approach to the slightly elevated green. Playing to par on the final three holes is a noble accomplishment.

Besides some very good golf, Tomahawk is a great walk unspoiled. There are no houses, no condos, no malls, and no fences. Just golf among the hills and trees.

"The Old West"

Turquoise Valley Golf Course

NACO, ARIZONA

February 14, 1912, is the date on which Arizona became a state. Appropriately, it quickly became known as the Valentine State. But, approximately five years prior to that, the game of golf was introduced to the Arizona Territory. And just as southeastern Arizona is rich in the history of the Old West, it also has a surprisingly rich golf history.

Naco, Arizona, sits right on the United States–Mexico border about 10 miles from the historical Western town of Bisbee. Because of its rugged terrain and somewhat remote location, you would not suspect that this area would be the first hotbed of golf in Arizona. The original course in the Bisbee area was constructed in 1908 in the Warren District just a few miles from downtown Bisbee. It was fittingly named the Warren District Country Club. The course was rudimentary at best, with gravely fairways and

Opposite: Old-style golf architecture is well demonstrated from the sixth tee.

oiled, sand-based greens. The location was about 5 miles from where the present course is now located. The first true golf professional at the club was William "Willie" Marshall, a Scotsman who arrived in 1909. Interestingly, the game was not exclusively the domain of the male population despite the area's rough-and-tumble lifestyle and the fact that golf was a new experience for southwest Arizona. In the clubhouse today you can find a picture of the 1910 Warren District Women's League, with ladies dressed in the golfing regalia of the day.

Around 1930, Phelps Dodge, the major mining conglomerate in the area, saw the need to expand its operations onto land near the golf course. Since it was the dominant political and economic force in the area, the course was forced to relocate. A new venue was sought and in 1931, the Newells, a prominent local family, donated property in Naco within 300 yards of the border with Mexico. Notably, the property was deeded with the stipulation that it always remain a golf course, a specification that still stands.

Construction began on a nine-hole course in 1936 under Franklin Roosevelt's Works Progress Administration (WPA) and opened the following year. The name of the course became the Turquoise Valley Golf Course.

The course remained under the domain of the city until 1991 when Loren Brewer, a Montana cowboy and professional rodeo rider, became its next operator. Brewer purchased the buildings and leased the course from the city. He left his mark on the property by constructing the first fifty sites in the RV park directly across the street and upgrading the golf course.

The third is a short but dangerous par-3. A pond, bunkers, and a large willow guard the green.

Brewer continued to operate the course until 1996, when Peter and Leslie Lawson purchased the course, the buildings, and a portion of the surrounding land to the north and west. The Lawsons were Canadian sheep farmers and beef jerky entrepreneurs who were taking time off in the winter of 1996–1997 to travel in their motor home. Along the

The par-3 eighth requires length and accuracy.

way they were directed to Bisbee, Naco, and eventually the Turquoise Valley Golf Course. A one-week stay led to one month, and soon Peter Lawson was sitting in Loren Brewer's office making an offer. A deal was struck, and the Lawson's took over operation of the facility.

"The Old West"

One of Lawson's initial undertakings was to develop a second nine. He commissioned local golf professional Dick Atkinson to design it, specifying a par 6 for the new layout. Atkinson set to work, and the back nine opened in January 1999. Lawson also upgraded the irrigation system and completely remodeled the clubhouse.

This intriguing background leads to one distinguishing chronological fact: Turquoise Valley Golf Course is the oldest continuously operating golf course in Arizona. For golfers with an appreciation of golf history, this is a must play.

The course features four sets of tees presenting a challenge for players at any level of ability. The back (black) tees play to a yardage of 6,778, requiring the advanced player to execute quality golf shots, while the forward (red) tees test the ability of the more relaxed player. The layout of the two nines is diverse. The older front nine are typical of layouts from the golden age of golf design, featuring small greens with a pronounced slope from front to back or side to side. All of the holes play either uphill or downhill and have fairways of moderate width bordered by cottonwood and fir trees, creating the illusion that the fairway is narrower than it really is. Unfortunately, the identity of the architect has not been preserved. Legend has it that the design was a collaboration by WPA workers who were also golfers. If that is the case, they provided a charming nine holes that require a variety of club selection for approach shots.

The most intriguing holes on the front nine are the two par 3s, numbers three and eight. The third plays to a maximum of 126 yards and requires a tee shot over a pond to a green that slopes dramatically from back right to front left. A large willow tree guards the left side of the green, forcing the player to hit a high shot or play to the right side of the green. The strategy required on the hole is appropriate to the challenge since the short yardage will require a lofted iron off the tee.

The eighth is a dramatic 223-yard par 3 that begins at an elevated tee, plays over a valley fairway, and finishes at a two-tiered, elevated green guarded on the left and right by bunkers. The hole demands accuracy and distance.

The back nine meander through the mesquite trees of the high Sonoran Desert and are almost totally flat. The length is considerably shorter than that of the front despite the fifteenth hole—the 747-yard par 6, which is nicknamed the "Rattler." Despite being shorter, the fairways are wider; however, the penalty for missing the fairway is much more severe than on the front nine. The greens are larger than those on the front by about one third, incorporating more levels and undulations. Two par 4s, numbers ten and twelve, are drivable for long hitters, but will punish an errant tee shot.

Two other holes, the visually spectacular par-3 eleventh and the eighteenth, require the tee shot to carry over Greenbush Draw, a 20-foot-deep ravine. In the 1950s in the Greenbush Draw a player looking for balls discovered the first Clovis point embedded in a mammoth bone. The Naco kill site is one of the oldest proven sites of man's existence in North America, dating back to 9950 B.C. The artifacts from the site are now located in the University of Arizona Museum in Tucson. The eleventh plays 198 yards from an elevated tee and requires a carry over Greenbush Draw. In the background are the high desert and the mountains. The green is large and rolling and guarded by two bunkers on the left side.

From the tee on the par-3 eleventh you'll have a great view, but a daunting tee shot over Greenbush Draw.

The most intriguing and most talked about hole is the "Rattler." It is virtually straight for the first 647 yards, with the fairway squeezing in at the landing areas. But at the 100-yard marker it turns 90 degrees to the right to a large sloping green guarded by water on the right side. This hole is the longest in Arizona and is reported to be the longest hole west of the Mississippi.

For avid history buffs, the area is chock full of historic sites. Closest are the remains of Fort Newell, where General Black Jack Pershing staged his Buffalo Soldiers before searching for Pancho Villa. And a museum in the town of Old Bisbee is the only Smithsonian affiliate in the country. It contains the most complete history of Bisbee and the surrounding area.

Turquoise Valley is truly off the beaten cart path. The closest interstate or four-lane highway is over 60 miles away. But the best golf is often in the most unexpected places.

Conclusion

SEARCHING FOR THE SPIRIT OF GOLF

The exploration for courses in *Off the Beaten Cart Path* was more than just research for a book. It was also a quest to uncover the spirit of the game. We, of course, were not the first to venture into this territory. A number of volumes about the spiritual and metaphysical aspects of the game have been written. We just approached the journey with a slightly different modus operandi. This different perspective gave us a unique advantage.

The heart and soul of American golf can be found at the courses that you have read about in this treatise. Of the sixteen thousand courses in the United States, the vast majority are like the ones you have read about here. They are not part of a golf resort. They are not part of a golf trail. They do not have overindulgent marketing budgets. What they do have is good, genuine golf. They are simply community golf courses played day in and day out with great pride by the local linksters. Seldom are there strict dress codes. You probably won't find a pair of FootJoy Classics on anyone's feet. You won't observe any golf bag with a major club manufacturer's logo neatly embossed on the side. During your round you may find that T-shirts, shorts, and sneakers are the attire of the day. But no one is really concerned.

Likewise, the people at these courses are the heart and soul of America. They may not have the greatest skill. They may not have the most technologically advanced equipment. But the one thing that they all have is the spirit of golf. They all enjoy the game and the camaraderie of their friends. And they are always thrilled to show off their courses. Those who play the game off the beaten cart path are concerned that you enjoy yourself while you are at their "homes." It is not a forced or imposed cordiality. Most assuredly it's from the heart: an I'll-do-anything-for-you attitude, a real enthusiasm for the game of golf.

The spirit of this enchanting and mysterious game that we love to play is a subjective entity. It is difficult, almost impossible, to define. In a 1999 video appropriately entitled *The Spirit of the Game*, the United States Golf Association defined it as observing the rules and etiquette of the game. But this is only a small part of the puzzle. There is so much more to it. We searched to discover the infinite number of missing pieces.

One fact we can quickly ascertain: the spirit of the game can be perceived a lot more easily than it can be defined. You can see it, hear it, and feel it, but it's hard to put it down on a piece of paper. In our travels across the United States it was easy to recognize it when it presented itself, but sadly, it was not equally manifest at every golf course. At some courses it was in full bloom, but at others the seeds needed to be replanted. There are those employed by the game—the luckiest people in the world, though many do not realize it—who are so deeply involved with the business that they lose sight of the true spirit of the game. But the good news is, despite the adverse influence from those who take to the game for profit only, that spirit was always in evidence somewhere. It may be difficult to ascertain. It may not be recognizable to everyone. But it is always present. But you just might require a certain sensitivity to recognize it.

When we came to know the story behind Rochelle Ranch Golf Course in Rawlins, Wyoming, it was plain to see. We did not have to wait long for people to share the story of their course and their pride in it. The Rochelles donated $7 million for the development of a course in their hometown, a place they never left, at least not spiritually. The golf course was truly a gift—the ultimate manifestation of the spirit.

We encountered the spirit in Garner, Iowa. The proprietor of Garner Country Club graciously telephoned his father-in-law, who immediately came to the course to tell us its story. You see, he had once owned the land where the golf course now stood, and willingly parted with some acreage for the good of the town.

We found it in Van Horn, Texas, at Mountain View Golf Course. When we walked into the back room of its clubhouse, two friends, one African American and one Mexican American, were watching a golf tournament on a small television mounted in a corner of the room. And when we explained our mission and inquired about the possibility of playing, we got a warm reception and their undivided attention.

In Chamberlain, South Dakota, we called at noon to inquire about playing. "Sure, if you can be here by one," we were told. "Today is ladies' day." When we arrived, the ladies were sharing a bit of birthday cake. We, of course, were invited to partake. The rest, as they say, is history. And plenty of information about the course was volunteered.

The spirit of golf comes in many forms and is generated in many ways. You can tell if it's there. You may not always be able to put your finger on what it is, but somehow, when you do find it, you know it. The golf course and everything around it generate that spirit. That is why we searched out the story of each course: for within that story is the spirit of the game.

Index